Understanding Your Inner Child and Overcoming Addiction

T0372836

This book provides a comprehensive overview of the Inner Child Model™ for treating Addictive Behaviors, a trauma-based approach to the treatment of various addictions including alcohol, drugs, food, gambling, sex, spending, smoking, etc.

Research indicates the onset of addiction is impacted by childhood trauma, inability to process emotional discomfort, and attachment disorders. This book addresses each of these issues to assist individuals in overcoming the drivers of addictive behaviors. But more importantly, it provides solutions to help those who struggle to learn to manage their addiction. It contains numerous case studies in which readers will see themselves and their stories throughout the pages and assists readers in generating a comprehensive recovery roadmap that will provide real-world solutions to staying one step ahead of their addiction. While there have been books written about the Inner Child, few focus on how the Inner Child impacts addiction. This unique and interactive therapeutic approach empowers individuals by assisting them in understanding "why" they engage in addictive behaviors.

This book is written for anyone struggling with behavioral/substance addiction, their loved ones, and clinicians working in the field of addiction treatment.

Eddie Capparucci, Ph.D. LPC, C-CSAS is a licensed counselor certified in treating Problematic Sexual Behaviors. He and his wife, Teri, have a private practice working with men struggling with sex and pornography and their wives dealing with betrayal trauma. He is the creator of the Inner Child Model™ for treating Compulsive Sexual Behaviors. He has worked with professional athletes among his many clients, including NFL and MLB players and television personalities. He is the administrator of the websites www.MenAgainstPorn.org and www. SexuallyPureMen.com. He has also written for Covenant Eyes, KingdomWorks, XXXChurch, and Marriage.com. Over the years, he has spoken to numerous organisations regarding the harmful impact pornography has on individuals, relationships, and society. Dr. Capparucci also is the author of the book *Why Men Struggle to Love: Overcoming Relational Blind Spots.*

Nathan Jones, MBACP (Accred) BA, PG DIP CBT, ICRPS is a BACP-accredited psychotherapist who specialises in the treatment of substance and sexual addiction. He is the Clinical Director and Founder of the London Centre for Addictions. Nathan entered residential rehab in 2012 and has been in recovery ever since. He has additionally trained as a Cognitive and Behavioural Psychotherapist and is a Certified Inner Child Recovery Process specialist. Nathan runs treatment groups for sexual addiction and substance misuse. He is currently completing his professional doctorate in the treatment of substance and sexual addiction at the University of Central Lancashire. Nathan provides training for clinicians on the Inner Child Recovery model and has presented at international conferences on pornography addiction and the erosion of attachment.

'Insightful, compassionate and well written. Should help to ease an often unrecognized source of much distress.'

Frederick Toates, *professor, author of*
How Sexual Desire Works: The Enigmatic Urge

Understanding Your Inner Child and Overcoming Addiction

A Recovery Manual and Workbook

Eddie Capparucci and Nathan Jones

Routledge
Taylor & Francis Group

LONDON AND NEW YORK

Designed cover image: © Getty Images

First published 2024
by Routledge
4 Park Square, Milton Park, Abingdon, Oxon OX14 4RN

and by Routledge
605 Third Avenue, New York, NY 10158

Routledge is an imprint of the Taylor & Francis Group, an informa business

© 2024 Eddie Capparucci and Nathan Jones

The right of Eddie Capparucci and Nathan Jones to be identified as authors of this work has been asserted in accordance with sections 77 and 78 of the Copyright, Designs and Patents Act 1988.

All rights reserved. No part of this book may be reprinted or reproduced or utilised in any form or by any electronic, mechanical, or other means, now known or hereafter invented, including photocopying and recording, or in any information storage or retrieval system, without permission in writing from the publishers.

Trademark notice: Product or corporate names may be trademarks or registered trademarks, and are used only for identification and explanation without intent to infringe.

British Library Cataloguing-in-Publication Data
A catalogue record for this book is available from the
British Library

Library of Congress Cataloguing-in-Publication Data
Names: Capparucci, Eddie, 1957- author. | Jones, Nathan (Psychotherapist), 1983- author.
Title: Understanding your inner child and overcoming addiction : a recovery manual and workbook / Eddie Capparucci and Nathan Jones.
Description: Abingdon, Oxon ; New York, NY : Routledge, 2024. | Includes bibliographical references and index. |
Identifiers: LCCN 2023014229 (print) | LCCN 2023014230 (ebook) | ISBN 9781032523026 (paperback) | ISBN 9781032523033 (hardback) | ISBN 9781003406013 (ebook)
Subjects: LCSH: Substance abuse. | Substance abuse--Treatment.
Classification: LCC HV4998 .C367 2024 (print) | LCC HV4998 (ebook) | DDC 362.29/18--dc23/eng/20230626
LC record available at https://lccn.loc.gov/2023014229
LC ebook record available at https://lccn.loc.gov/2023014230

ISBN: 978-1-032-52303-3 (hbk)
ISBN: 978-1-032-52302-6 (pbk)
ISBN: 978-1-003-40601-3 (ebk)

DOI: 10.4324/9781003406013

Typeset in Times New Roman
by MPS Limited, Dehradun

Contents

Chapter 1

Pathway to Addiction

Let's start with a simple confession. *"I am an addict."* Repeat it, but this time aloud. *"I am an addict."*

That sucked, didn't it? Nobody wants to surrender control of their lives to an addiction. But you already have. Think of all the wasted energy, time, and money you invested in your addiction. The opportunities and relationships lost or damaged. If we could slow down the negative noise in our minds for a moment, we would recognise how pathetic our situation has become. But the noise is loud, unforgiving, and challenging to manage.

Accepting we have an addiction leaves us feeling defective, shamed, and warped. It makes us feel dirty. Add to that the thought of others judging us as weak-minded, and we may as well be draped in a shame blanket.

Our undesired behaviors keep us trapped in the vicious, destructive cycle, leaving us agonising over why we cannot stop the madness. After years of failing to manage our addiction, we begin to believe there is not much hope of ever becoming clean.

For as long as we can remember, our addiction of choice has been the epicenter of our lives, be it substance or behavior. We waste hours pursuing it. And once we have it, we cannot stop indulging. There never seems to be enough, and worst yet, there's no shut-off valve. What we love the most, we hate the most. Being trapped in our addiction is like hell on earth.

Creating Healthy Children

Most people can indulge in pastimes such as drinking alcohol, gambling, eating, smoking, having sex, and using social media without allowing these activities to lure them into a world of torment. So, what makes these individuals different from those of us who battle with addictions? There are several factors:

- They are emotionally developed and, as children, were taught to identify, process, and express their emotions in a healthy way.
- They learned to effectively process their emotional pain and discomfort instead of running from it using various distractions.
- They were not subjected to or had limited emotional, mental, physical, and sexual traumas or neglect and therefore do not have many unresolved childhood pain points that continue to haunt them today.

Creating Unhealthy Children

The circumstances are quite different for those caught in the web of addiction. Unlike their healthy counterparts, instead, they were not:

DOI: 10.4324/9781003406013-1

- Provided with a safe environment but instead endured abuse and/or neglect (dealing with unresolved childhood pain points).
- Taught how to sit and process emotional discomfort but, rather, learned to escape using behaviors that could lead to addiction (inability to process emotional pain).
- Provided nurturing and guidance to attune, empathise, and trust others, as well as how to identify and express their emotions (becoming emotionally undeveloped).

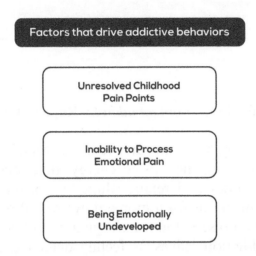

Can you identify similarities you experienced with the three factors listed above that drive addictive behaviors? Each represents an unhealthy environment in which children receive little or no instruction or guidance on how to bond emotionally and connect. Simultaneously, they are subjected to trauma and neglect that leads to an anxious lifestyle. For the most part – unlike their counterparts – these kids grew up with a strong need to escape emotional distress experienced as children or teenagers. And today, as adults, they are still running.

The Pathway

I (Nathan Jones) am a recovering drug addict who developed a pathological relationship with alcohol, cocaine, and mephedrone (M-CAT). I began drinking when I was 17 and quickly realised one was "too many" and a thousand "not enough."

My behavior resulted in an arrest for possession of cocaine, a DUI, and bankruptcy. I caused tremendous anguish for my loved ones and hurt many people during the chaos of my addiction. On August 1, 2012, I entered a rehabilitation unit and began to explore the root of my addiction.

I soon learned I suffered from an attachment wound that inhibits the ability to bond emotionally. When I was 11, my parents divorced, and I was distraught. I can still remember my terrible loss as our family was torn apart. That said, I recall always wanting more of everything as a child; chocolate, video games, clothes – whatever I could get, so maybe there was also a genetic element to it. Perhaps, I was always destined to become an addict.

This attachment wound made me subconsciously develop the worldview that *"I must please people so they don't leave me"* and *"if I make people laugh, they will like me."* The fear of rejection and abandonment underpinned my worldview and made me a people-pleaser and the village idiot.

I began using alcohol and drugs to fill the emotional void within. It started a ten-year addictive cycle, which brought me to my knees and almost killed me and others. Once I identified and processed the unresolved childhood pain points that drove my addictive behavior, the conditions for the drug use were removed, and I could make healthier choices. Today, I am married to my beautiful wife, Sofia, and we have an amazing daughter, Jasmine, and I have finally escaped the clutches of addiction. Today, I am free.

The pathway to addiction did not begin when we exited the womb – although some born to mothers who abused drugs suffer from addiction symptoms upon birth. Instead, for most of us, the foundation for addiction began long before our first high, and its roots are anchored in our childhood. Unfortunately, those at risk of addictive behaviors swim in a pool of unresolved childhood pain points that the subconscious mind will do anything to keep repressed.

OUR REAL PROBLEM IS NOT THAT OUR WOUNDS ARE HIDDEN, BUT THAT THEY HAVE NEVER BEEN HEALED

While fleeing emotional pain is one of the key factors of addiction, a vast majority of those addicted don't understand they act out to accomplish this objective. They are oblivious to the rationale behind the tragic actions that are destroying their lives.

Their addiction serves as a coping mechanism, which allows them to avoid dwelling on the past emotional pain points that shaped their lives as children. These might include abandonment, abuse, bullying, physical appearance, lack of affirmation or attention, rejection, etc. The list goes on and on.

These unpleasant childhood pain points often manifest into adulthood attachment wounds, from which we seek relief by engaging in coping strategies to help us avoid the emotions we fear. We learn that numbing, withdrawing, disconnecting, or disassociating are all effective methods to avoid dealing with our past traumas or neglect.

The Pain That Lasts a Lifetime

Anthony grew up in an athletic family, including a father who played professional football. His older brothers and younger sister were star athletes throughout middle and high school. On the other hand, Anthony lacked the coordination required to excel in sports. This resulted in his father overlooking his athletically challenged son to instead focus on the children who shared his athletic ability. Anthony felt rejected and believed he wasn't worthy of his father's love. His dad never laid a hand on him and rarely raised his voice in anger. Instead, he acted as though Anthony did not exist. Anthony experienced neglect at the hands of his father, the very person who was supposed to provide him with unconditional love and acceptance. And that is a very difficult existence for a young child.

To escape the mental distress of feeling unloved and judged by his father, he turned to alcohol at the age of 15. Getting drunk provided an escape from the exhausting anxiety of believing he didn't meet his dad's expectations and that he was inadequate.

This is just one example of the self-destructive behavior we may engage in to seek relief from our emotional distress. And in turn, these behaviors constantly repeated, serve as the gateway to the development of addictions. As they become mainstays in our lives and we return to them repeatedly, these behaviors form entrenched addictive neural pathways that change and alter our brain chemistry by increasing dopamine levels and other hormones responsible for generating pleasurable emotions. Over time, this process ultimately increases the risk of those behaviors becoming addictive.

For Anthony, whose negative self-narrative was *"I am a disappointment,"* the goal was to generate a state of hypo-arousal to numb his emotions. And he accomplished this by abusing alcohol. The more he leaned on drinking to deaden the critical voices in his head, the stronger his reliance on the substance became. Alcohol provided temporary relief from the knowledge that his father would never provide him with unconditional acceptance and validation.

As an adult, whenever he sensed he was not meeting someone's expectations, Anthony would head off on a multi-day bender ignoring all responsibilities. Of course, in time, this action led to serious relationship and employment issues.

While Anthony chose to numb his childhood pain points, others engage in behaviors or use substances that increase arousal to generate feelings of control or power. *"I was tired of feeling nothing,"* said Stanley, who lived in foster homes for eight years after his mother died of an overdose when he was eight. The coping strategy of choice depends on whether an individual wants to either shift from numbness to experiencing euphoric emotions or move away from their distressful feelings and experience numbness. And the options available to do this are endless.

The Importance of Why

Working with those who struggle with addiction, we often hear clients moan about how they landed in this cesspool called addiction. *"I don't know how I got here. I cannot understand why my addiction started. I know when it began, but I cannot tell you why I allowed it to manifest in my life."* One of the key objectives of this book is to provide insight to help you and your loved ones understand *why* you are trapped in addiction.

So why is *why* so important?

We're glad you asked. When we understand *why* we think, feel, and act the way we do, we become empowered to make substantial and long-lasting changes in our lives. This knowledge allows us to deal rationally with adverse circumstances while simultaneously moving away from irrational, often self-destructive, emotionally-based thinking. Having insight into your struggles provides the ammunition required to make healthier decisions.

There is a root at the base of all addictions, and in many cases, it is formed around our unresolved childhood pain points. Here are a few examples. (BTW, the case studies in this book are real; however, the names and some of the details have been changed to maintain our clients' anonymity.)

Sally

Sally was a well-adjusted 14-year-old with an active social life. She received good grades and was a force on the athletic field. Then one day, Sally's entire life changed. Her parents announced they were getting a divorce. An only child, Sally was devastated because she had never seen any dissension between her parents. They were gentle and loving toward each other and seemed the epitome of a couple in love.

But it was all a deception. Sally later discovered they had never loved each other and only got married because Sally's mom became pregnant. Her parents agreed to do their best to provide Sally with a loving and comfortable home, which they did for 14 years. But behind the scenes, there was no intimacy between them.

Finally, Sally's father reached the point where he could not live in the fabricated environment any longer, and he had an affair, which ultimately led to him telling his wife he wanted out of the marriage.

All of this shocked a young girl who thought her life was perfect. Her initial pain eventually turned to anger, so to escape her loss, she started using weed at 15. By 16, she was sexually active, drinking daily and popping amphetamines. By 17, she had dropped out of school and solicited older men to support her crack habit.

What was at the core of Sally's addiction? The emotional pain of realising her life was a façade. This made her doubt everything about herself and who she was as a person. It also led her to question reality in general. She did not know what was real and what was not. The emotional turmoil was too much for the young teenager to handle, so she elected not to think about it, instead choosing to distract herself with drugs and alcohol.

Josiah

Josiah's father was a lifer in the Air Force. This meant Josiah and his family moved throughout the world every 18 to 24 months. As you can imagine, making friends was difficult when he didn't know how long he would be around. By eighth grade, Josiah had given up trying to make friends. The disappointment of leaving behind newly found buddies became just too difficult to endure.

So at 14, Josiah found himself an alternative friend who would always be available and provide hours of entertainment – pornography. With his father deployed for months at a time, and his mother struggling with alcohol, Josiah had little supervision, allowing him to slip easily and unchallenged into the world of porn, escaping the reality of his loneliness and isolation.

Throughout his high school years, Josiah became more reclusive, leaving the house only to attend school and little else. He put on nearly 50 pounds in weight and started to become depressed. By the time he left for college, he was a committed loner and would continue that lifestyle until he entered therapy in his late 30s.

At the core of Josiah's addiction was low self-worth and tremendous self-loathing. He concluded that friends were not to be had because there was something wrong with him. People were able to see the ugliness inside him and stayed away. These lies kept him entrenched in pornography, which was now the only source of comfort for a very lonely man.

Courtney

Courtney was daddy's little girl, and the two had an enormous bond stolen when her father was killed in an auto accident. At only nine years old, she was devastated by a loss that was compounded by her mother shutting down any discussion about the tragedy.

With no outlet to allow her to deal with her sense of abandonment and grief, Courtney found comfort in sniffing glue. The rush would make all her daddy pain disappear for a while, which was a welcome relief. As she worked her way through middle and high school, she continued experimenting with various narcotics, including meth, in her senior year.

In addition, Courtney also sought a replacement for her father through older men. Starting at 14, she would scroll the Internet seeking male companionship. What began as random chats would turn into sexual hook-ups with more than 35 men over three years. For Courtney, these encounters were failed attempts to relieve the abandonment pain she experienced following her father's death.

And with each disappointing sexual encounter, Courtney turned ever further toward drugs to numb her feelings of loneliness and shame about her promiscuous lifestyle.

The Open Wound

The inability to understand *why* we engage in addictive activities leaves our core wound untreated. It is like an open sore that remains infected, destroying not only our entire bodies but also the lives of our loved ones.

I have been dealing with her selfish and reckless behavior for years, said Samuel about his wife, Theresa. *Yes, I knew she liked to drink when we started dating, but I never thought it would get to the point where she would go on week-long benders and not come home. We have three children who need their mother.*

But you will not find her at home focused on them, he continued. *No, you are more likely to find her in a bar in the middle of the afternoon or passed out in the basement. And I cannot understand why she does this to herself and her family. Why?*

Millions of men and women have stories like Courtney and Theresa. They are lost souls who cannot find an escape route from the addictions that are tearing them and their families apart. Instead, they remain stuck in a cesspool that perpetuates feelings of shame and disgust. And they believe there is no way out.

Pulling at the True Root

Those struggling with addiction (and those who love them) commonly believe the root of the problem is a weak character. *"I often feel like I am not strong enough to deal with this eating disorder,"* said Terrance, whose obesity has led to diabetes. *"I know my family feels that way. They are constantly on my case to simply control my food intake. It seems easy, but I cannot get it right. And they do not understand what I go through."*

Individuals like Terrance deal with overwhelming shame, believing the root of the problem is a lack of willpower. But I will let you in on a secret. That answer is incorrect. And without a clear-cut rationale for *why* we struggle, we will default to believing the issue is a character flaw or lack of willpower. Read what Connor, who struggles with sex addiction, has to say.

"I am convinced I am hard-wired differently than other guys," as he explained his habit of spending nearly $250 weekly on live sex webcasts. *"There is no other explanation for why I am consumed with sexual thoughts around the clock. I can't get them out of my head."*

Connor is right; he is hard-wired to abuse sex, but not due to a character flaw. Connor's obsession with sex was developed as a coping strategy to counter the emotional distress people and events had caused him at a young age. Connor learned to block out emotional anguish by engaging in distracting activities to protect himself. And at some point, his go-to distraction became sex.

To straighten out his wiring, Connor – like all addicts – will benefit from uncovering the true root of his addiction and the core emotional triggers that activate it. To do this, he will need to go deeper to answer the **why** question.

"If you want to understand why you are addicted to something, you have to understand the conditions that keep your addiction in place," writes Jay Stringer, a counselor, ordained minister, and author of the book *Unwanted*. *"The choice of unwanted sexual behavior is never accidental. There is always a reason. Your path to freedom from destructive behavior begins with finding the unique reasons behind yours."*

Well said.

Understanding the roots of your addiction will empower you, whether you are just starting your recovery journey or have been on the path for some time. When we know the rationales for our poor behaviors, we can put ourselves in a position where we are more likely to make wise decisions when temptations lurk. Listen to Dr. Capparucci's story.

Loved Ones Are Not Dependable

I am a recovering sex addict whose issue centered on womanising. Since the time I started dating, having one girlfriend was not enough. At the time, I did not know why this was the case; all I knew was, being with one girl for too long was uncomfortable.

My behavior resulted in two divorces and tremendous pain for many who did not deserve it. Shortly after the breakup of my second marriage, I sought a therapist's assistance to understand the root of my problem.

What we soon discovered was that I had suffered from an attachment disorder (an avoidant attachment), and so, unknown to me, I always had one foot in and one foot out of all relationships. My avoidant attachment disorder prevented me from letting anyone get too close for fear of being abandoned. So, when and where did that fear develop?

When I was five, my father died suddenly of a heart attack, and my mother had a nervous breakdown which required her to be hospitalised for nearly a year. I was sent off to live with relatives I did not know, and no one was telling me what had happened. You can only imagine the fear going through the mind and body of that little boy, uprooted from his home, and living among strangers.

This attachment wound resulted in my subconsciously developing the worldview that *"those who say they love you are undependable. And those who say they love you will leave you."*

There is much more to the story, but the point is, until I understood *why* sex had a stronghold on my life, I was destined to repeatedly make the same tragic mistakes. Once I identified and processed the unresolved childhood pain points that drove me toward infidelity, I was able to make fundamental changes in my life. I am happy to say I have been married to my current wife, Teri, for 25 years, and I have been faithful the entire time. Not something I should need to brag about, but I will.

Their Need for Empathy

As you read this book, you will understand that discovering the origin of addiction is vital in the recovery process. The key to unlocking the power of addiction is for individuals to uncover why it manifested in the first place. Answers to the *why* question provide relief and the hope that we will be able to manage our addiction. And this is the alternative to shame and frustration.

Remember, this is not a solo journey. Your loved ones need to know the answer to the *why* question too! Knowing *why* you engage in reckless behaviors will allow them to understand what triggers your addiction and help them support you in long-term recovery.

When loved ones understand *why*, it opens the door for them to develop empathy, which is vital to building trust and mending past wounds. This powerful emotion enables loved ones to see the addict through a softer pair of eyes – eyes that are not so condemning and judgmental.

In developing empathy for an addict, loved ones indicate an understanding of the problem. They are not saying they accept the behavior in any way, shape, or form. They will continue to despise it. But by becoming empathetic, they, too, can find healing.

A mother whose 20-year-old son repeatedly stole from her and physically assaulted her on one occasion when high sat with him and his counselor on his first sobriety anniversary. During the session, she told her son, *"It's taken years, but I finally understand the emotional pain that drove you to drugs. And it breaks my heart you went through such pain at a younger age, and I didn't know it. But you must understand I will never forget the torment you caused me during your addiction. Your actions still hurt me, but I am working on forgiving you."*

True Remorse

Understanding the rationale for their compulsive actions does not give addicts a free pass. And they certainly cannot use these insights as excuses or to gain sympathy. Instead, they must take full responsibility for the pain they have caused others.

"It's a relief to understand the reasons behind my sexual addiction," said Billy, who ran through three marriages due to his expensive escort habit. *"But that doesn't change the fact I have messed up and hurt people, especially my ex-wives. That's on me. I own that."*

Individuals like Billy must commit to recovery while demonstrating the desire to transform and change their hearts. Those who own their actions are ultimately the ones who will succeed in this battle. These people show:

* Deep understanding of the harm they have caused
* True sense of remorse
* Hunger for insight into the origins of their compulsive behaviors
* Passion for the pursuit of ongoing recovery
* Willingness to participate in a community with others who struggle
* Desire to deepen the emotional bond with their spouse, family, and in some cases, God
* Commitment to develop a servant's heart and put the needs and desires of others before themselves

Moving beyond the Behavior

You are about to embark on a journey in which you will not merely attempt to change your destructive behaviors but, more importantly, embrace and achieve integrity. Your recovery will focus on consistent personal self-reflection to understand better *why* you think, feel, and behave the way you do. The Inner Child Model will launch you on a mission to change your heart, which goes far beyond managing your addiction. Your aim is to become a new man or woman.

However, this approach involves sacrifice, and the only sacrifice addicts are willing to make allows them to indulge in their addiction. The mighty quest to obtain a rush to counter numbed emotions, or quiet painful ones, flies in the face of decisions based on integrity.

Changing your life is a major undertaking filled with gratification, accomplishment, excitement, and happiness. But more importantly, these life-altering changes will move you from merely existing to living your life.

But understand this: knowing *why* your addiction manifested is NOT the only insight and strategic tool you will need to manage your disorder. However, in our experience, it is the driving force that will empower you on this recovery journey. And this new sense of empowerment will allow you to employ the necessary tools to manage your addiction successfully.

"While healing does not occur by knowing exactly how and why the addiction developed, it does come when the addict learns to put these experiences into perspective by acknowledging how these experiences have had an impact," writes Dr. Kevin B. Skinner in his book entitled

Treating Pornography Addiction: The Essential Tools for Recovery. "*Then, with this knowledge, he will know how to do things differently in the future.*"

Dr. Skinner points out the importance of understanding why and how the answers to this question can change our decision-making process. Whenever we act out, it correlates to a core emotional triggers. Remember those three words – core emotional triggers. These words are critical to the Inner Child Model, and we will refer to them repeatedly throughout this book.

Need to Identify Core Emotional Triggers

Often, we fail to identify core emotional triggers when they occur and subsequently become engulfed in destructive behavior. Why? Because we are not aware of our core emotional triggers. Also referred to as hidden triggers, they are based on subconscious emotional pain points. By failing to pinpoint and understand why we are entrapped in addictive behaviors, we limit our ability to uncover the solution to manage them effectively. But you don't know what you don't know.

Without vital information, it is difficult to solve any problem we face. For example, doctors can't adequately heal patients until they make a correct diagnosis. And that is our focus – embarking on a journey to diagnose the cause of our addiction, starting with answering the *why* question. This answer will lead us to uncover those important core emotional triggers.

Sex addicts are not born; they are created. Over the years, we have understood that individuals who endure trauma/neglect early on – including physical, emotional, mental, or sexual abuse – are more at risk of turning toward addictive behaviors and substances.

We have also learned that addicts struggle to deal with difficult emotions because they are fear-based. They are afraid of confronting pain points from the past when these subconsciously crop up through events happening in our current lives. The truth is they are scared of, once again, experiencing those awful emotions. Most importantly, we have uncovered another vital factor that is the primary driver of all addictions.

The Inner Child.

Workbook

Objectives

While there are many things you will learn about yourself and your addiction as you go through the workbook, there are two main goals you are seeking to accomplish.

Goal Number 1: To understand why your addiction has a stronghold on your life.
Goal Number 2: To transform your heart, rebuild your life and provide you with a sense of peace.

So how will you achieve these goals? We're glad you asked. Here is the game plan.

1   You will start by obtaining insight into yourself and, most importantly, begin answering the *why* question: "*why* do you think, feel, and act the way you do?" This journey of understanding and enlightenment will help you stay one step ahead of your addiction.

   Therefore, as you walk through this workbook, do not cut corners. Be as detailed as possible with your answers. You will be asked to return to your childhood and explain the circumstances. This won't be easy. Consider it the first test of your newfound ability to sit and process emotional pain points.

THIS IS AN EXTREMELY IMPORTANT POINT:

   Complete these exercises through the eyes of your younger self and not through the eyes of you as an adult. As an adult, you will attempt to rationalise what occurred. When you were a child, you could not rationalise hurtful events. Your views were based on *emotional* thinking and not *logical thinking*. So, you must stay focused on the younger you when doing this work.

2   Give your Inner Child a name. Most individuals who go through this process add the word "Little" before their name, "Little Robert" or "Little Sarah." Feel free to be more creative in deciding how you will refer to your little one, but remember, although the child is a driver in your addictive process, he/she is not bad. Your Inner Child is simply scared and seeking comfort. So, be gentle and loving, and treat the child as you wish others had treated you.

3   Be honest with yourself. We know there are many things you feel ashamed of, including events that occurred when you were a child. But you are no longer a child. Today is the start of becoming an emotionally mature human being, which means being transparent and honest. Yes, confronting some of our past hurts can be very difficult, but it is necessary if we want them to stop haunting us today. You can do this.

4   You may struggle to remember your past. This is not uncommon for those who have dealt with abuse or neglect. Journalling is one of the most effective tools to help jump-start your memory. You should also reach out to other family members to get their insights on what occurred when you were growing up. You may want to go right to the source of where you think the issues lie, including parents, siblings, or peers, and confront them with compassion to see what information you can gain. Again, take this process slowly, and do not be like a bull in a china shop in your attempts to get answers.

5   You might feel enormous guilt while trying to understand how your parents may have failed you, but this is perfectly normal. Look at it this way. We are not saying your parents were bad people; they simply did not have the necessary skills to assist in your emotional growth and development. Many parents who struggle with addiction also possess low emotional IQs. So, as you uncover how their flaws impacted you, you might

want to throw your parents under the bus. But once the process is over, you can pull them back out again with a better understanding.

6 Spend time thinking about the person you want to be. What qualities would you like to have? Start drafting a document outlining what you want your legacy to be when family members and friends talk about you. Work with your support group members and sponsor to get their feedback on your ideas. The sky is the limit, so dream on and set out to be transformed.

How does dealing with your addiction **make you feel**?

Check all that apply

A Exhausted ☐
B Frustrated ☐
C Hopeless ☐
D Powerless ☐
E Shameful ☐

Explain the reason(s) for your answer:

_____
_____
_____
_____
_____

Despite these feelings, you are making the brave decision to get insight and go deeper! Congratulations.

1 "The road to recovery from addiction runs through your childhood." What do you **already understand about your childhood**? How would you describe your childhood?

_____
_____
_____
_____
_____

2 Write a description of the people who had an **impact on your life**. Describe the good, bad, and ugly about each of them, including any abuse and/or neglect. Try to be objective.

Dad

_____
_____
_____
_____
_____

Mom

_____

_____

_____

_____

_____

Siblings

_____

_____

_____

_____

_____

Others

_____

_____

_____

_____

_____

3   What do you want to **understand better about your childhood**?

_____

_____

_____

_____

_____

4   Which of these statements best **describes you**?

A   I did not witness a healthy model of intimacy displayed by my parents that I was able to replicate □

B   I have experienced emotional, mental, physical, or sexual traumas □

C   I was not taught to identify, process, and express my emotions, including hurtful and painful feelings □

D   I don't understand why I think, feel, and behave the way I do □

E   I was neglected □

F   I learned to objectify women/men instead of admiring their appearances □

G   I don't know how to identify my true emotions, and I have trouble expressing them □

5   Take time and **explain why** you chose the answers to question 4.

_____

_____

_____

_____

6   How do you believe it would assist your recovery if you could **understand why** addictive behaviors have a stronghold on your life?

_____

_____

_____

_____

_____

7   What **types of traumas** did you endure while groing up?

   A   Emotional   ☐
   B   Mental   ☐
   C   Physical   ☐
   D   Sexual   ☐
   E   None of the above ☐

8   What specific experiences can **you recall** regarding those traumas?

_____

_____

_____

_____

_____

9   **Why** do you believe you are trapped in your addiction? (Make a guess.)

_____

_____

_____

_____

_____

10   Why are you currently **pursuing freedom from addiction**?

_____

_____

_____

_____

_____

11   What are **the barriers** you believe keep you from successfully managing your addiction? Be specific.

_____

_____

_____

_____

_____

12   Do you believe you have **taken full responsibility** for the hurtful actions you have engaged in, including lying and deceit? If yes, write down what you have taken responsibility for. Is there anything you may not have owned regarding your behavior?

_____

_____

_____

_____

_____

13   Part of recovery is achieving personal integrity. What would **achieving personal integrity** mean for you and your loved ones?

_____

_____

_____

_____

_____

14   While this may not be a fair question at this stage, can you **identify some of the Core Emotional Triggers** that lead you to engage in addictive behaviors? We will compare these answers later after you have finished this workbook.

_____

_____

_____

_____

_____

15   Well done! Now **comment** below: what are two key points you have learned in this chapter, and how do you believe they will influence your recovery? Be as specific as possible in your answers. Remember, you are seeking to gain insight into yourself.

_____

_____

_____

_____

_____

Chapter 2

Understanding Your Inner Child

Before we discuss the Inner Child, let us take a moment to point out that this treatment method is only one of many therapeutic approaches that may be required to assist you in managing your addiction, depending upon its severity.

While the Inner Child Model is extremely effective in helping those who deal with addiction, depending upon the severity of the disorder, it should be used in combination with other therapeutic approaches. For example, if you deal with substance addiction, you may need detox before engaging in Inner Child work or long-term care in a residential program. Teaming up with a nutritionist first would be highly beneficial for those struggling with eating disorders. Support groups are also a must-have for anyone in recovery. Having a support team of individuals who have already taken the journey and can serve to encourage you along your road to recovery. Identifying the appropriate treatment plan for you should ideally be done with the assistance of an addiction specialist.

Who Is This Kid?

As you start to dig deeper into this book, you are probably asking yourself, *"Who is the Inner Child, and how could he/she possibly have anything to do with my addiction?"*

And frankly, we do not blame you for thinking such a thought. The concept of the Inner Child is nothing new. However, little effort has been made to apply this therapeutic approach to helping individuals struggling with addiction. So, let us briefly examine who this child is and why it would benefit you to get to know the "little one" better.

Your Inner Child is representative of your subconscious emotional and mental pain and is derived from people and events in your life that resulted in trauma and/or neglect. Your Inner Child, who has experienced frightening and confusing moments throughout your young life, sits in the background of your subconscious. And while these children may produce a constant, low-level grumbling of anxiety in some of us, their actual presence is felt when they become activated by core emotional triggers. See, we told you to remember those three words.

As we said previously, the Inner Child concept is nothing new. Many philosophers and mental healthcare professionals have discussed and debated it for centuries, and many aspects of the Inner Child have been thoroughly reviewed and written. However, using the Inner Child to treat addiction is a unique and exciting approach that offers much hope for those struggling with these disorders.

Charles Whitman wrote an excellent book entitled *Healing the Child Within*, which examines many dimensions of Inner Children, including their playfulness. However, this book will focus on a single component of the Inner Child – emotional pain. Why? Because we believe, in part, the child's unresolved emotional distress leads individuals to turn to addictive actions for relief or reward.

DOI: 10.4324/9781003406013-2

We also believe the Inner Child cannot be healed. Instead, those struggling with addiction need to learn to **manage** their Inner Child. Why is this the case? If you suffered trauma and engaged in therapy to treat your mental and emotional wounds, you realise that trauma is never completely removed from your life. Instead, the pain is desensitised, and you are taught coping strategies to help you deal with future triggers.

In Dr. Capparucci's Inner Child Model for treating addiction, the kid's pain is still active. Therefore, managing the negative emotions we present when triggered is up to us. Prior to learning to manage our Inner Children, we allow their emotions to drive us to escape the anxiety or discomfort we feel by engaging in addictive activities. But with the knowledge you gain by implementing the Inner Child Model, you no longer need to pander to the kid's fears. You are the one who will be in charge, and with that will come great confidence and non-indulgence. And that is exactly what your Inner Child desires – for you to take charge and provide protection.

Two Worlds Collide

But how can unresolved pain from our past lead to addictive behaviors? Because the Inner Child correlates the adverse events and circumstances you face every day with painful memories of past events, which appear remarkably similar to him/her. To make matters worse, in many cases the child's interpretation of current circumstances does not always match up with the painful events of the past. But to the Inner Child, it seems that way, which leads us into trouble.

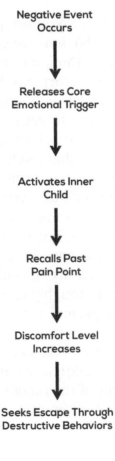

The Activation Process

Negative Event
Occurs

↓

Releases Core
Emotional Trigger

↓

Activates Inner
Child

↓

Recalls Past
Pain Point

↓

Discomfort Level
Increases

↓

Seeks Escape Through
Destructive Behaviors

For example, your wife asks you to stop by the store to pick up milk, but you leave your brain at work and forget to stop at the store. When she asks, *"Where's the milk"* your brain returns, and you realise, *"oops."*

Before you can even apologise, she yells and says how selfish and inconsiderate you are. You try to defend yourself, but her sharp sword is no match for the white handkerchief you are waving. And while the yelling is terrible enough, she does something that activates your Inner Child, she walks out of the house and heads to the store.

While you are annoyed at yourself for not paying more attention to your chore list, this leaves your Inner Child screaming. Why? Because when you were a child, every time your mother got angry, she would punish you by exiting the room, leaving you feeling abandoned. It was a tactic she knew would make you worried she would never return. And so the milk event has left your inner kid correlating your wife's *current* behavior to your mom's *previous* behavior. Two worlds have collided – the present and the past. And it's never pretty.

We will share more about the connection between past and current circumstances when we get to the Inner Child Activation Process Chart later in this chapter.

The Kid Is a Runner

It is essential to understand that while our inner children are very fearful, they are also extremely powerful. They taught us to use distraction and withdrawal coping strategies to avoid uncomfortable emotions. And in many cases, they go a step further to protect themselves by putting up walls to conceal these complex and hurtful emotions. Our inner children are runners. They run and hide to pretend the emotional pain doesn't exist.

The problem is, when they run, they take us along with them. So we, too, have learned to be runners, seeking an escape to distract us from what we should be doing – processing emotional pain that is part of human lives.

Knowing your Inner Child is locked in a time warp is essential. He/she is forever at ground zero, reliving various painful events you suffered as a child or teen. The kid is surrounded by scarring memories such as dad referring to him as a "little girl"; dealing with school bullies; a slap across the face by her mom; freezing in front of the class when giving an oral presentation and hearing the laughter and taunts; being the last one selected in gym class; watching dad shove mom during another night of fighting; your brother sexually abusing you; being told you are stupid or not pretty; the list goes on and on.

During this journey, you will discover your Inner Child is exceptionally selfish – but not because of his/her own doing. You see, the child was not taught how to process complex and troubling feelings. As children, if we don't receive guidance and direction on managing and processing the disappointing and unsettling things in our lives, we will learn to ignore all painful circumstances by turning toward behaviors that distract our attention and provide stimulation or numb us.

This is a central problem with our inner children; they are super sensitive and easily triggered by negative events. And when these kids get started (basically, they are having a tantrum), it leads to bad decision-making for you if you are not mindful of what is happening.

Oh, we forgot! Those who deal with addiction aren't mindful. Can you see the potential dilemma?

Our inner children do not think about others' feelings or the consequences of their actions. That is why when a wife asks, *"What leads you to turn to pornography so often when you have me available,"* she often gets the answer, *"I don't know."* Your Inner Child is not concerned with your wife's or anyone else's feelings, for that matter.

What the Inner Child Wants

Our inner children only have one goal – to seek comfort. They are locked in survival mode and will do anything to avoid experiencing the troubling emotions endured in the past. And to avoid feeling, they have learned to use various – and sometimes destructive behaviors – to distract and self-soothe.

Remember, the emotional chaos your Inner Child experiences is extremely powerful and very frightening. Therefore, these children require an escape outlet to overcome their pain levels. They seek relief or reward, which is where addictive behaviors and substances come in. The adrenaline rush provided is so effective it can help to mask any emotional distress.

How? By increasing these addictions of neurochemicals and hormones in the brain. Dopamine, serotonin, norepinephrine, and oxytocin are neurotransmitters the body naturally produces. Addictive behaviors result in higher levels of these pleasure-seeking chemicals being generated, and this results in the production of a rush or high. When we engage in the same behaviors repeatedly, such as snorting cocaine, binge eating, viewing porn, or drinking excessively, our bodies and minds develop an unhealthy craving for these neurochemicals and become obsessed with obtaining them.

Once your Inner Child stumbles across this chemical method for easing pain thresholds, it is like leaving the child alone in a candy store. He/she will increasingly want more. The key for us will be to **stay one step ahead** of the child before there is a meltdown and we are sent off running to obtain a rush. The Inner Child's objective is simple – *"I need to do whatever will help me feel safe."* Again, can you see the potential problem we face?

You must become more alert and mindful to manage the kid and stay one step ahead of your addiction.

Inner Child Taking Over

Let us take a moment to demonstrate how the Inner Child impacts your addiction. This is referred to as the Inner Child Activation Process, which results in the kid running the show and causing grief for us and those who love us.

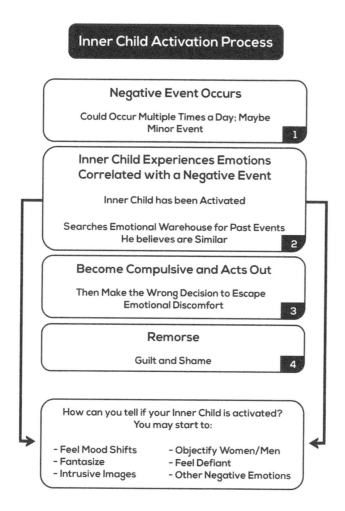

Starting at the top of the diagram, our troubles begin when negative events occur in our day-to-day lives (Stage 1). These events, ranging from inconvenient to disastrous, could happen multiple times throughout the day. In some cases, we might easily dismiss them. But if the event correlates with a core emotional trigger that haunts your Inner Child, there could be real trouble. Here's an example.

You are looking for a parking space with your family at the shopping mall. You see one, but just as you are about to pull in, another car cuts in front of you and grabs it. You are annoyed but keep moving along until you find another spot. Once in the mall, along with your wife and kids, you start shopping, trying not to think about the rude driver.

End of the story, right? Wrong. While you are attempting to dismiss the event, your Inner Child has other ideas. He has correlated the incident in the parking lot with being bullied in school and not standing up for himself (Stage 2). He feels weak and humiliated, just like he did when kids picked on him.

If you were to hear some of your Inner Child's negative self-talk, it would probably sound like this. *"Why didn't we do something when he cut us off? We never stood up to anyone in school. They would push us around and take our lunch money. We're weak and pathetic!"* And there is your core emotional trigger – *"I feel weak and pathetic."*

The Inner Child in Action

Your Inner Child is activated when this occurs, which is not good. But how do you know the kid is starting to throw a tantrum? Easy. He wants to run away and forget about what happened. He wants to escape the emotional distress. So, what does he do? He engages in the same strategy he has been using for years. He makes you feel discomfort. In turn, this may make you experience anxiety, tension, irritability, numbness, anger, boredom, etc. And, when you experience these troublesome feelings, you are programmed to seek out a distraction – which usually involves your addiction of choice, in this example, sex.

Let us continue with our story at the mall. While you are unaware your Inner Child has been activated, you find your mood shifting (Stage 3). You tell yourself you are getting tired and bored. But because you are unaware of your true emotions (feeling weak and pathetic), you probably aren't connecting the shift in mood to what happened in the parking lot. Instead, you may blame it on being at the mall when you could be home watching the football game. As your mood shifts downward, you tell your wife you need a break from shopping and you are going to sit down.

After a few minutes, you start paying more attention to the women walking past. Being a "breast man," your eyes lock in on the assorted sizes of breasts – large, medium, small. One by one, you check out the breasts of every woman who walks by you. You are lost in space and time and have forgotten where you are. You're dissociating. The only thing in your world at that moment is the exploration and study of breasts.

Your Inner Child has achieved his objective. He is no longer focusing on the emotional turmoil that resulted from the parking lot incident and past bullies, but he has stopped you from feeling weak. Instead, you now feel empowered.

The hunt for breasts has served as a significant distraction, and thanks to the rush of neurochemicals your brain is experiencing, you are in la-la land. Even your Inner Child has become quiet, feasting on the sights in the mall. And when your family finishes shopping and says they're ready to go, you won't even know how long they have been gone.

The Inner Child Activation Process runs quietly in the background and can be kick-started numerous times during the day. The depth of your mood change can range from unnoticeable to dramatic. But it doesn't matter. If your addiction involves food you may have found yourself gorging at the food court. If your struggle is alcohol you may have found your way to a seat in the mall pub. If you are unaware of your Inner Child and the pain triggers, you will be subjected to acting out every single time he is activated.

The Inner Child in Action II

Let's look at another example of the Inner Child Activation Process, this time checking in on Ann after she receives a call from her supervisor, Carol, complaining about a project.

Ann:	*"Guess I will start reworking those numbers for Carol."*
Ann's Inner Child:	*"I hate her. She is never happy and always complains about one thing or another. There is nothing we can do to make her happy."*
Ann:	*"I thought I did a good job on that report."*
Ann's Inner Child:	*"We're an idiot for trying to please her. No matter what we do, women like her will not be happy. She's just like Mom, who thought we were useless."*
Ann:	*"Now that I think about it, she's not being fair."*
Ann's Inner Child:	*"We need to go to Jimmy's Tavern to forget about her and her crazy assignments. We deserve that."*
Ann:	*"I think I will take a break."*

Can you imagine where Ann ended up? Yes, it is not hard to figure it out. But once her bender at Jimmy's is over, she will beat herself up, wondering, *"How did I end up there?"* It underscores the Inner Child's power in heightening Ann's emotional state. While it is ok that Ann is upset with Carol, the intensity of her frustration increases because her Inner Child added to the emotional distress by bringing mom into the equation. And Ann is not consciously aware the dialogue with her Inner Child occurred. All she knows is her anxiety has steadily increased as she thought about the interaction with her boss. Let's review how this all played out.

Instead of recognising the core emotional triggers that resulted from Carol's call (*"I am not good enough"* and *"I am a disappointment"*); and then putting her effort into processing those emotions, Ann becomes a runner, following the lead of her Inner Child. She doesn't sit with the emotional pain caused by Carol but instead escapes to Jimmy's Bar, which serves as a useful distraction – at least until the hangover kicks in.

The Inner Child Is Part of the Self

Not understanding her Inner Child (or even realising she has one) makes it impossible for Ann to slow down the kid. Therefore Ann has yielded her power to her Inner Child without recognising what the kid is doing. Side note – when we yield our power, bad things happen.

Unfortunately, like Ann, most of us are unaware our Inner Child exists. And there is a good explanation for that, as described by Dr. Donald Price in his article, "Inner Child Work: What Is Really Happening?"

"The Inner Child is not just a visual image or metaphor, but a powerful and influential part of the self," explains Dr. Price. *"However, the Inner Child may not be accessible through conscious exercises. The Inner Child is explained as a non-associated or dissociated and often disowned or disavowed part of the self or self-representation; it has some degree of ego-state formation and is state-dependent. It is a mental unit or structure of varying degrees of complexity or development, depending on the individual person, and often has the power to exert passive influence on the conscious state."*

Ok, that was heavy stuff. What the good doctor is saying is inner children are buried in our subconscious. Therefore we are unaware of their presence, and because of this, they can create significant trouble in our lives.

The Inner Child Offers Clues

Again, this doesn't make our inner children bad. They are scared and confused and prone to react in emotionally charged ways. But there also is an incredibly positive aspect of our inner children. They can serve to assist us in identifying our genuine emotions in any given circumstance. Matt Price (no relation to the above Donald), in his book Inner Child: *Find Your True Self, Discover Your Inner Child, and Embrace the Fun in Life*, points out the positive nature of engaging our Inner Child.

"As we continued to mature, we learned to put on different masks or facades. We have learned to hide how we feel to avoid unpleasant encounters in life, such as pain, bitterness, rejection, and disappointment," says Price. *"While these defense mechanisms serve a healthy purpose to protect ourselves, we sometimes become detached from our true selves because of this fear. Sometimes these true feelings get bottled up and stowed away in some corner inside of your mind until they grow to become so big that you will eventually burst and crack. The Inner Child can help you recover from this habit of holding it all in by letting you accept how you genuinely feel."*

"For instance, many individuals have cheated because they hide their feelings of having 'fallen out of love.' They had to wait until they were tempted before they listened to their Inner Child, which has led them to inflict pain and sorrow upon another," he continues. *"This would have been avoided if the person had acknowledged how he or she felt about his or her partner beforehand. The Inner Child can point out these true feelings and then enable the adult side to handle the situation maturely."*

Not Knowing the Child Exists Is Our Downfall

Our risk of inappropriately acting out increases dramatically when we are not aware of the presence of our inner children and what core emotions trigger them.

Dr. Stephen A. Diamond, writing an article for Psychology Today entitled *Essential Secrets of Psychotherapy: The Inner Child,* points out that a triggered Inner Child can lead to unimaginable chaos.

"We were all once children and still have that child dwelling within us. But most adults are quite unaware of this," said Dr. Diamond. *"And this lack of conscious relatedness to our Inner Child is precisely where so many behavioral, emotional, and relationship difficulties stem from."*

Now, this is a critical point you should not miss. Your Inner Child is a challenge because you are unaware of him/her. And that is a BIG problem. In fact, when it comes to our addictive behaviors, it is the biggest problem of all. Our lack of awareness regarding the existence of the Inner Child is our downfall because we have been subconsciously trained to follow the child's lead without asking questions.

"These so-called grown-ups or adults are unwittingly being constantly influenced or covertly controlled by this unconscious Inner Child," continues Dr. Diamond. *"For many, it is not an adult self-directing their lives, but rather an emotionally wounded Inner Child inhabiting an adult body."*

Are you starting to get the picture? To manage your addiction, you need to know your Inner Child. But believe it or not, it is an exciting process learning about the kid and what makes him/her react and the core emotions that trigger the child. What triggers your child depends on the extend of the trauma, neglect and trying circumstances you faced as a child. The clients we work with develop close-knit relationships with their inner children and often create nicknames to describe the kids.

"Dr. Eddie, you will not believe what Little Boo tried to get away with this week," explained Betsy, 52, who endured a long struggle with alcohol and crack. *"She is a handful, but I am working hard to stay one step ahead of her."*

"Nathan, young Donny was screaming at me to use today," exclaimed Donald, who was being treated for his addiction to methamphetamines. *"Thankfully, I could stay one step ahead of him and use my 'wise mind' to regain control."*

Comforting your Inner Child can be challenging because the child's goal of avoiding emotional pain flies in the face of successful recovery. To help manage your addiction, you need to learn to sit and process emotional discomfort instead of seeking unhealthy distractions in an attempt to make them go away.

However, this is not a natural reaction for those who deal with addiction. It is a skill you will need to develop.

How Did the Kid Get This Way?

It would be helpful to take a brief look at how our Inner Child developed into a fear-based kid. But first, let us review the conditions children MUST have to ensure healthy emotional development.

* We need nurturing. This includes attention and affirmation. As children, we long to be wanted and desired. Knowing we are loved and that someone is there for us is critical. This sense of belonging is vital in developing healthy self-worth.
* We need structure. We require rules and discipline. When our parents provide us with structure, we feel valued. They are providing us with the guidance and protection we need to survive. Without it, we sense we are on our own and will grow up to be inwardly focused.
* We need stimulation. A child's brain is like a sponge that craves interaction and knowledge. It is natural for children to seek adventure and excitement to help develop curiosity and a sense of autonomy. When a child is not stimulated or challenged to explore and learn because of neglectful parents, their intellectual and emotional growth becomes stifled. Basically, no one teaches them how to live and love.
* We need insight. Our caregivers are responsible for helping us put words to our emotions, so we do not rely solely upon anger and withdrawal to deal with difficult circumstances. Instead, we should be able to identify our true emotions and healthily express them. Many who deal with addiction also struggle to connect emotionally, which can be linked to the lack of nurturing and guidance during the early stages of childhood development.

When children are denied development in one or more of these areas, they will experience uncertainty and anxiety, resulting in a frightened Inner Child. A lack of nurturing will lead kids to question their values and self-worth. Since they are not being loved and affirmed, they will see themselves as the problem and believe they are unlovable. And without a guardian helping them to process the emotional issues that arise in childhood, these kids learn to avoid discomfort via distractions. And there begins the establishment of addiction roots.

The Lasting Wounds

Being egocentric, children have difficulty blaming parents who do not demonstrate love and affection. A child cannot see a situation from another person's point of view and therefore assumes others feel the same they do. So, in a child's mind, there is only one explanation for why mommy and daddy do not love me – *"there is something wrong with **me**."*

In his book, *Homecoming: Reclaiming and Healing Your Inner Child*, John Bradshaw discusses how the Inner Child's identity is hindered by wounds inflicted during his early years.

"The wounded Inner Child contaminates intimacy in relationships because he has no sense of his authentic self," says Bradshaw. *"The greatest wound a child can receive is the rejection of his authentic self. When a parent cannot affirm his child's feelings, needs, and desires, he rejects that child's authentic self. Then, a false self must be set up."*

Without structure, children do not feel secure or develop the ability to master self-discipline. Parents who set up routines and boundaries for their children communicate the message, *"I care, and you are important. You can feel safe with me."*

When no structure surrounds children, they deal with a constant fear of the unknown. This lack of protection is terrifying for kids who live with uncertainty and do not know what to expect daily. Lack of structure also prevents children from learning to discipline themselves. Since there are few rules, and it seems no one cares, why should the child? Worst yet, this kid is less likely to reflect on the consequences of his actions. This makes it more likely he will engage in risky behavior. Oh, wait, that sounds like an addict!

And there is another negative repercussion derived from a lack of consistent and healthy parenting. Since the child grows up believing no one cares, he must take it upon himself to provide his own caring and nurturing. This results in him turning inward and looking out for himself first. Because if he does not care for himself, who will?

Our Low Emotional IQ

When we lack stimulation as children, we are set up for failure as adults due to being deprived of various sensory stimulations that limit our brain development. And nowhere is the lack of stimulation more relevant than in the development of an individual's emotional IQ. In our clinical practices, nine out of ten individuals who present with addiction also have a low emotional IQ. The consequence of this is three-fold:

1 They can tell you when they are angry, sad, happy, or afraid – these are all *primary* or instinctive emotions – however, they struggle to identify their genuine emotions, which are called *secondary* emotions. For example, they exhibit anger, but the real emotion driving their anger may be feeling disrespected.
2 Usually, if they can identify true feelings (secondary emotions), they cannot constructively articulate them. They struggle to share because they fear being dismissed, criticised, or told their emotions are invalid. They consider vulnerability a dirty word.
3 But worst of all, they cannot determine what others feel beyond primary emotions. They cannot empathise and seek additional information from others expressing their feelings. Instead, they seek to shut down the individual, fix the problem, or minimise it to reduce their own anxiety.

While your Inner Child experiences emotions (a vast majority being painful), the child does not know how to process those emotions or how to soothe him/herself. Because they were never taught how to manage negative feelings successfully, they elect not to feel at all by developing distractions (running away).

In her book *Running on Empty*, Dr. Jonice Webb points out how children suffering from neglect learn to cut off their emotions to protect themselves, resulting in adults with low emotional IQs.

"When you grow up with your parents failing to notice what you are feeling, you are growing up with the most powerful expression of your deepest self (your emotions) ignored.

What is a child to do?" she writes. *"Fortunately, and unfortunately, children's brains automatically step in to protect them in these situations.*

"When, as a child, you perceive, on some level, that your emotions are not welcome in your family, your brain automatically walls them off for you," she continues. *"This way, those troublesome feelings won't burden you and your parents. In many ways, this coping technique is brilliantly adaptive. But it's also what makes you feel empty as an adult."*

The inability to deal with negative feelings and engage in real emotional intimacy is partly responsible for keeping the addict spiraling uncontrollably into dysfunctional relationships.

"Growing up and moving forward in your life, you are unaware of what your brain has done for you," Dr. Webb continues. *"You are not aware of your blocked feelings. You are unaware that you are living your life without full access to a key life ingredient that everyone else has: your emotions."*

The Devastating Impact of the Inner Child

As we mentioned before, being unaware of our Inner Child and his/her core emotional triggers is like walking in the dark. Sooner or later, you are going to fall into a pit. Dr. Charles Whitfield, the author of *Healing the Child Within*, confirms that our inability to understand what triggers our Inner Child can lead to severe consequences, causing deep emotional and mental distress.

"When the child within is not nurtured or allowed freedom of expression, a false or co-dependent self emerges," he says, *"we begin to live our lives from a victim stance and experience difficulties in resolving emotional traumas. The gradual accumulation of unfinished mental and emotional business can lead to chronic anxiety, fear, confusion, emptiness, and unhappiness."*

What Dr. Whitfield doesn't explain is the *"unfinished business"* we experience can lead to our Inner Child seeking out destructive behaviors, may result in addictive activities.

Dr. Esly Carvalho agrees with the concept that our Inner Child is strongly connected to past trauma/neglect, much of which we have erased from our conscious thought process.

"Unhealed traumatic experiences eternally repeat themselves inside of us. This repetition doesn't end because the brain stays actively connected to our unprocessed memories," according to Dr. Carvalho in her book, *Healing the Folks Who Live Inside*.

"Our brain stays in a state of hypervigilance because the deep brain continues to feel the need to protect itself from perceived danger," she continues. *"It is as if our mind does not 'know' the danger has passed, so it continues in high alert, in an anxious state, always concerned that something bad is going to happen. Somebody inside continues to live and relive the traumatic experience."*

As we pointed out earlier, your Inner Child is locked in a time warp, so you must learn to manage him/her effectively. The child is trapped forever in those years when you endured trauma or neglect, leaving repressed emotional scars. However, your Inner Child intimately knows every emotional wound you endured in your early years. The child can recall messages received either directly or indirectly from parents, siblings, peers, and other authority figures that produced emotional and mental harm. The child has memorised every negative narrative that you hold onto today. The child forgets nothing, which makes the kid a challenge to manage.

Negative Narratives

Negative narratives (or negative self-talk) are unfavorable beliefs you inflict upon yourself. They play ever-so-softly in your head, so softly, in fact, you can barely hear them. The following are examples of some negative narratives:

- You Don't Deserve Love
- You're A Bad Person
- You're Worthless
- You're Not Lovable
- You're Powerless
- You're Invisible
- You're Not Good Enough
- You're A Mistake
- You're Always Wrong
- You're Ugly/unattractive
- You're Stupid
- You Don't Belong
- You're A Failure
- You're A Disappointment
- You're Defective

These are only a handful of the destructive lies we learned to believe about ourselves at the hands of the people and events that hard-wired us as children. When an adverse event occurs in our daily lives (Stage 1), it may remind the Inner Child of a negative narrative, which will cause the child to be triggered (Stage 2). For example, one of your co-workers, Carol, walks right by you in the hallway without saying hello (Stage 1). You find it curious because Carol is one of the friendliest women in the company, but you tell yourself she was probably distracted.

However, your Inner Child is not taking the same rational approach to sort out what happened when Carol walked by you. The child immediately jumps back to previous times when others ignored you (Stage 2).

"I remember when Beth turned everyone against us in third grade, and we didn't do any-thing wrong. The other kids walked by us and didn't talk to us for the last six weeks of the school year. We felt left out. You can't trust people who say they like you!"

Your Inner Child has had years to replay the trauma and neglect you endured as a kid. Because of this, she is fear-driven and reactive. She relies solely on emotional thinking to deal with the circumstances you face today and often misreads them, ultimately causing unnecessary emotional and mental distress.

Go back to Carol for a moment. You are sitting at your desk and cannot concentrate because you feel Carol is upset with you – that you've done something wrong (Stage 3). But a moment later, she pops her head in your office and says, *"Want to hit the café for a cup of coffee?"* Carol's actions have cut the activation cycle short, dramatically reducing your risk of turning toward your addiction for relief or stimulation.

Your Inner Child may have been triggered by Carol not acknowledging you, but her conclusion was wrong. That is what happens when we react by focusing solely on the emotional-thinking skills of our Inner Child. To have a fighting chance of not turning toward your addiction, you must shift from *"what you feel"* (the Inner Child's emotions) to *"what is real."* And what you will find in most cases is that what you feel and what is real are two entirely different things.

Stage One: You Experience a Negative Event
Stage Two: Your Inner Child is Activated
Stage Three: Your Risk of Acting Out has Increased

Our Inner Child is driven by emotional thinking because, as a child, it was the most advanced skill he/she had available when facing a crisis or conflict. Their analytical and cognitive capabilities were not fully developed, leaving them to make assumptions based on raw emotions and limited worldly experiences. They had limited use of the critical, analytical, or concrete thinking skills that we as adults use to help us assess troubling situations and make rational decisions. These inner children were, and still are, alone and in the dark, trying to navigate a world they don't fully understand – and the result often brings more pain and uncertainty.

As you can imagine, the Inner Child's perception of things may not match reality because of this dilemma. The child is a highly reactive fellow who runs on impulse. It is strictly a reactive urge to act without thinking of further consequences. In fact, he/she believes the course of action selected – escaping and seeking adrenaline rushes – will bring pleasurable results. Unfortunately for us, the child is wrong.

It Is about Past Pain

In his book *Unwanted,* Jay Stringer points out addictions are created through the entanglement of two worlds.

"How did I get here?" he writes. *"One way of thinking about unwanted sexual behavior is to see it as the convergence of two rivers: your past and the difficulties you face in the present."*

To take his brilliant word picture to the next level, consider your Inner Child's river (which comes from your past) as muddy and dreary. When the child reacts to current events (your river) in your world, the child's highly overreactive nature starts to pollute your river by heightening your discomfort (anxiety) level. All the mud and debris from past emotional pain comes roaring into your current river, leaving you dealing with negative feelings and, worse still, not understanding how they got out of control.

You see, your Inner Child is responsible for telling you an event has occurred that will change your mood (and not for the better). To the child, the current circumstance has become strikingly like past traumas/neglect, and the kid has been triggered. In turn, you also have been triggered – although you may not be aware of it at the time. (Again, refer to the Inner Child Activation Process Chart for how this occurs.)

Harry's Story

Let's look at another example. Harry and three other design team members are called to the boardroom by the company CEO, who announces they have won a new client thanks to their hard work. Although not intentionally, when the group gathers, three members sit on one side of the table, and Harry sits alone on the other side. When talking with the team, the CEO looks exclusively at Harry's counterparts, gushing with praise and affirmation. Realising he has left Harry out, he turns to him and, with a slight grin, says, *"You did a good job, too"* (Stage 1). Harry nods and smiles. But something is wrong.

The CEO glanced and grinned at Harry, causing "Little Harold" (the name Harry gave his inner child) to experience the emotional pain of being left behind and unnoticed. Little Harold now feels like an afterthought.

Little Harold immediately recalls when dad told Harry's twin brother Larry how proud he was for driving in the winning run during a Little League game. Although Harry had three hits that game, Dad merely looked at him and gave a quick grin before turning his attention back to Larry. It probably was not his father's intention to slight Harry, but that is what happened. And this occurred on more than one occasion. Harry often felt he played second fiddle to Larry regarding Dad's affirmation and attention.

"I was never as good as Larry," is what Little Harold remembers. *"Dad loved him better. And I know why. It was because I was a good athlete. I just wasn't good enough. I was never good enough"* (Stage 2). Harry's Inner Child is full of negative self-talk, and Harry is about to suffer because of it.

As Harry left the meeting, he forgot the situation and briefly celebrated the win with his peers, but for some reason, he was not in the mood to celebrate long. Instead, he justified his mood by telling himself it was no big deal to win a new client and that he needed to get back to work, which he did.

Later, he stopped at a massage parlor (Stage 3) and allowed a woman to masturbate him. Feeling disgusted after it was over (Stage 4), he wondered, on the ride home, why? It had been months since the last time, in which he had told himself, *"Never again!"* What Harry didn't know was Little Harold was running the show.

Isn't it interesting to see the correlation between your Inner Child's behavior and your behavior when it comes to your addiction? Both of you are:

- Highly emotionally charged
- Compulsive
- Not focused on potential consequences
- Trying to escape emotional distress

Yes, allowing your Inner Child to remain in charge of the show causes mental and emotional pain and grief. That is why we must get you empowered so you can take back control of your life and learn to manage your addiction effectively.

The Child Is Not Going Anywhere

Clients ask, *"When does the Kid leave me alone?"* The answer is never. Your Inner Child is not going away. The pain he feels does not diminish much over time. But he can be taught to adapt and put his trust in you.

The more you work to help comfort, teach, and protect, the more the kid will learn to trust you and your decision-making. The child will still be activated when a core emotional trigger occurs, but you will find it easier to get his/her attention and allow the child to give up control of the situation, permitting you to take charge. You will then be staying one step ahead of the Kid.

But it is an ongoing process. You will find the more mindful you become of your addiction, your Inner Child, and core emotional triggers; the greater success you will achieve in managing tempting situations as they arise. Mindfulness is a significant component of the recovery process, which we will cover in depth later.

It is crucial to remember we are not trying to discipline or shame our Inner Child. The children cannot control their emotions because they are stuck in a time where they experienced huge emotional and mental distress. No one taught them how to deal with stressful situations. Therefore, based on their limited life experiences, they had to sort through their trauma and neglect alone.

Imagine being 6 to 12 years old and trying to figure out on your own why dad does not pay any attention to you. No one is available to help you sort through the pain, hurt, and disappointment you feel. In most cases, you take responsibility, thinking there's something wrong with you, which is why daddy is ignoring you.

Getting in tune with your Inner Child deepens your self-awareness, a skill your kid lacks. This new skill set will allow you to stay alert to high-risk situations while helping comfort your Inner Child. In so doing, you ultimately will learn to manage your addiction.

Five Objectives

As we finish up Chapter 2 and prepare to meet the 11 kids, let us briefly review five points we want you to keep top of mind when reading the rest of this book.

1 Become aware of your Inner Child. Start the process by understanding what your child has gone through and his/her fears. Learn to empathise with the child despite the havoc the kid can cause in your life.
2 Identify and understand their core emotional triggers to limit how they negatively impact you. Many core emotional triggers could activate an Inner Child and push you toward launching into your addiction. That is why it is essential to determine what core emotional triggers activate your kid. This is accomplished in part by examining the cast of characters and events that negatively influenced your life.
3 Learn how to educate and comfort your Inner Child. Let the child know you are here to protect him/her. The child needs to understand an adult is available to guide the negative circumstances and that the child does not have to try to manage the scary pain alone. The kid also must understand that today's circumstances do not always correlate with suffering from the past. It may just seem that way.
4 Stop running away from the emotional pain impacting your Inner Child and instead learn to sit with hurtful emotions. This is a challenging step, but it is also the most critical step. We have been programmed to avoid emotional pain at all costs. But running away and trying to escape reality is not an option. Nothing good comes from turning away from your fears. There is a real benefit in confronting our pain, including helping us mature.
5 Although the kid has enormous power and influence, YOU are still responsible for your decision-making. And that will only happen when you decide to take control and become more mindful of yourself, your Inner Child, and your surroundings.

HEADS UP: As we move along, we will be sharing the *Inner Child Model* that will provide you with the ultimate solution for managing your activated Inner Child.

Workbook

1 How do you typically **deal** with emotional distress?

    A I run away from the distress   ☐
    B I pretend there is no distress   ☐
    C I slow down and process the distress ☐

2 What **humiliating or hurtful** moments can you remember suffering as a child? (As you start this process, don't be surprised if you discover memories long forgotten. It's ok! You're gaining valuable insight to help you manage your addiction.)

_____
_____
_____
_____
_____

3 Can you guess what **negative events** often activate your Inner Child?

_____
_____
_____
_____
_____

4 What **thoughts** and **feelings** are activated by those negative events? For example, "I feel weak and pathetic."

5 Which **negative narratives** (the lies you believe about yourself) resonate with you? Highlight the ones that trouble you.

I don't deserve love	I am a bad person	I am worthless
I am powerless	I am invisible	I do not matter
I am not good enough	I am a failure	I am stupid
I am unattractive	I am a disappointment	I am defective
I do not belong	I am always wrong	I am a mistake

Your negative self-talk is the result of lies fed to you since childhood. It is now time to face these falsehoods and set them against the truth of reality.

6 How do you believe these negative narratives **originated**? What messages did you receive as a child or teen, directly or indirectly, that go with the negative narratives you chose? This exercise is critical and the point at which you will begin your serious self-reflection, so please, be as detailed as possible in answering this question. If needed, use additional paper for your answer.

_____
_____
_____
_____
_____

7 Based on what you have been learning, how does your Inner Child **impact** your addiction?

_____
_____
_____
_____
_____

8 "Learn to comfort your Inner Child, and you will learn to manage your addiction." How much do you **agree** with this statement?
     0 = strongly disagree 10 = strongly agree

0	1	2	3	4	5	6	7	8	9	10

9 Which of these **objectives** are you most excited about? Explain.

   A Becoming aware of your Inner Child □
   B Identifying and understanding your Inner Child's Core Emotional Triggers □
   C Educating and comforting your Inner Child □
   D Learning to stop running from emotional distress that impacts your Inner Child and learning to sit with this distress □
   E Taking control and becoming more mindful of yourself, your Inner Child, and your surroundings □

_____
_____
_____
_____
_____

You have no control over your Inner Child being activated; how you respond to the child being activated is what you can control. You have more power than you think.

10 How will you respond the next time your Inner Child is activated?

_____
_____
_____
_____
_____

11 Which of the following aspects of recovery work do you believe could be **most beneficial** for you? Choose as many as you like.

A   Conducting a complete review of my sexual history/interests ☐
B   Identifying my negative narratives and learning to dispel them ☐
C   Processing past trauma and/or neglect ☐
D   Understanding healthy sexuality ☐
E   Doing emotional IQ work ☐
F   Developing a compassionate heart ☐
G   Bringing truth and change to every area of my life ☐
H   Identifying new passions ☐
I   Understanding the trauma I have caused others ☐
J   Various reading assignments ☐

12 Well done! Now **comment** below: what are two key points you took away from this chapter, and how might they help with your recovery? Be as specific as possible in your answers.

_____

_____

_____

_____

_____

Chapter 3

The 11 Inner Children

Before we meet the 11 inner children who comprise the Inner Child Model™, let us take a moment to reiterate this treatment method is only one of several therapeutic approaches that may be required to assist you based on the type of addiction and its severity.

We would stress that while the Inner Child Model is extremely effective in helping those who deal with addiction, it will often be used in combination with other therapeutic approaches. Identifying the appropriate treatment plan for you should be done with the assistance of an addiction specialist.

The role of the Inner Child Model is to provide you with the insights needed to identify the hidden core emotional triggers that are the driving force behind your inability to manage your addiction. This therapeutic approach will assist you in the following:

- Understanding the rationale behind *why* addiction has such a strong hold on your life
- Gaining insights regarding why you think, feel, and act the way you do
- Reducing compulsive behaviors
- Processing emotional discomfort
- Being more mindful
- Being empowered to stay one step ahead of your addiction

11 Inner Children, Numerous Triggers

There are hundreds of core emotional triggers that can activate your Inner Child and increase your level of discomfort. Through my (Dr. Capparucci) research, I identified 11 inner children, each based on emotional discomfort arising from unresolved childhood pain points.

These often-repressed pain points and the inability to sit with emotional discomfort frequently contribute to developing addictive behaviors. As you start this process of self-reflection to understand better *why* you think, feel, and act the way you do, it is important to note not all negative emotions impact your Inner Child. The goal is to identify those that lead to your kid's tantrums. With this insight, you will start building the toolbox you need to help disengage from compulsive actions.

Think of these 11 children as large buckets, and within each bucket will be more precise core emotional triggers. For example, the bucket entitled "The Unnoticed Child" contains more flushed-out triggers such as *"I don't matter," "I don't belong,"* or *"no one cares."* It will be necessary to drill down and be as precise as possible when identifying your core emotional triggers during the discovery process.

Finally, the following descriptions in this chapter are only brief overviews of each of the 11 children. We will review each kid in depth throughout the rest of this book. As you read,

DOI: 10.4324/9781003406013-3

we suggest you highlight or journal all the reasons that resonate most with you. Note that each bucket description may not match up entirely with what you experience. That's ok. The point is to identify any child who touches a raw nerve and makes you uncomfortable. Let the quest for insight begin.

The Bored Child

With the explosion of technology and numerous ways to entertain and stimulate ourselves, children are growing up believing they need to be doing something 24/7. Any downtime seems like wasted time. But having endless entertainment options at our fingertips is insufficient to overcome boredom. The antidote to boredom is being engaged in authentic relationships.

Individuals who associate with this child were often raised in environments with little positive interaction and stimulation with family members. Even if they came from a large family surrounded by people, they often felt isolated and alone. Therefore, they grew up learning to self-entertain, which led them to spend a lot of time in their heads. They may have had either no or just a few friends and spent much of this time alone, engaging in fantasy and self-play. They led a low-key and quiet existence as children and teenagers.

"I was bored out my mind as a child," recalls Janet, a married mother of three and small-business owner recovering from an addiction to opiates. *"My dad was always at the pub, and my mom ignored me. I found stimulation in boys and eventually my parents' alcohol cabinet."*

In the early stages of childhood development, these kids were not taught how to attune with others, be empathic, learn to trust, regulate moods, or identify emotions. This resulted in the development of individuals who struggled to connect with others and found it difficult to generate excitement in life.

That is, until addiction enters their world. Then everything changes, and not for the better.

The Unaffirmed Child

Imagine growing up and never or rarely hearing your parents or others say things like:

> *"That was an awesome job."*
> *"You're an amazing kid."*
> *"I think you're special."*
> *"You're very smart."*
> *"I enjoy spending time with you."*
> *"I am so proud of you."*
> *"You're fun to be with."*
> *"I love you."*

That is the issue facing an Inner Child who is starved of praise. These kids were raised in environments where they received little affirmation and/or probably over-the-top criticism. It left them feeling that nothing they did was good enough and wondering, *"what's wrong with me?"*

Growing up receiving few accolades – and perhaps a great deal of criticism – leads to low self-worth and a lack of confidence. These youngsters rarely had their achievements acknowledged or, worse yet, were told their efforts fell short. Even if they achieved success through academics or athletics, they believed their accomplishments were tainted or meaningless. As adults today, they brush aside compliments.

"I remember when I passed my teaching exam," recounts Jodie. *"I called home to tell my parents; I was thrilled with the news." "That's good, dear, but did you know your cousin Sarah is now a medical doctor,"* replied her father. *"I felt crushed inside and realised I could never do anything to be seen by my parents – I felt lower than a snake's belly."*

Since they cannot escape criticism, they turn to fantasy to create a world where they are always affirmed. Their daydreams center around being famous, influential, and well-liked.

Although they are chasing affirmation, these folks are often hypersensitive to criticism. Because of their sensitivity to being corrected, the praise they do receive is never enough. With every positive comment they get, a keen ear is listening for the criticism they are sure will follow. Their loved ones will often complain they are oversensitive and tend to withdraw and pout when someone is upset with them.

For this Inner Child, seeking praise is a bottomless cup that never gets filled. It leads to an endless quest for approval and recognition, resulting in destructive consequences.

On the other hand, the Unaffirmed Child may be the result of receiving an endless stream of praise and accolades. Whether for their athletic or academic achievements or their personal appearance, they were always the focus of attention and made to feel they were special and unique.

If one day that praise fades, these individuals will be on a continued quest to turn the spotlight back on themselves. And if this does not occur, there is a strong chance they will turn to addictive substances or behaviors to numb their disappointment.

The Unnoticed Child

One of the keys to developing healthy children is providing them with a sense of belonging. A child's understanding that they are accepted and desired is vital in creating solid ego strength and confidence.

But that is not how life pans out for kids who go through childhood and adolescence, never feeling they belong. Sometimes, they had to chase friends and family members to be included or noticed. These children were rarely sought out by others and would often wonder, *"what's wrong with me that someone would not go through the trouble of finding me?"*

Others were "drowned" out by family members or peers and felt they had no voice. It would not be uncommon for them to make comments that were ignored or glance over at the dinner table. This lack of attention made them feel rejected and invisible.

Like the bored child, this kid spent much time alone with thoughts, ideas, and worries, reluctant to share for fear of being dismissed or belittled. They developed an intense fear of rejection, which would keep them from taking risks in reaching out to others for engagement. One worldview this child experiences is *"it's safer to go it alone."*

This is especially true of those who report being bullied by siblings or peers. This type of trauma only increases the likelihood of children withdrawing and isolating, thus reinforcing the feeling they are not desired or wanted.

Jimmy is a firefighter who presented with an addiction to alcohol. He described his childhood as "systematic bullying." *"Every day at school, I faced physical, verbal, and psychological abuse,"* he said during one of his counseling sessions. *"I just wanted to fit in and be accepted. Instead, I felt like an outcast – always on the outside looking in."*

Jimmy described alcohol as his only friend. *"Alcohol was always there for me; never rejected me; never belittled me; never hurt me … until eventually, even the alcohol turned on me."*

Today, as adults, these individuals still crave to belong and possess a hunger to be pursued and feel desired.

The Emotionally Voided Child

Like the kid who received little or no affirmation, some children are raised where emotions are shunned, like COVID-19. Sure, there were expressions of anger, sadness, happiness, and fear, but deep-rooted feelings were off-limits.

These kids grew up with no model showing how to bond emotionally with others. Like the bored child, no one showed them how to identify, process, and healthily share their feelings. Instead, they were left to figure out how to deal with the emotional pain of scarring events.

Along the way, they received the message that *"feelings were not important – and perhaps dangerous."* To protect themselves, these inner children decided to stop feeling. They became proficient at suppressing emotions and locking them away in a black box, so they could never be reached.

The result? An adult with a low emotional IQ who has no idea how to emotionally bond with others. They have no clue what real emotional intimacy entails. Therefore, they cannot connect healthily and form meaningful relationships.

"I was often told to man up and stop acting like a baby," recalls Simon, who has been addicted on and off to cocaine for almost a decade. *"My father said that showing emotion was a sign of weakness, so I never learned to explore or express my feelings – instead, they were buried deep within me."*

Those with a low emotional IQ may find it uncomfortable to be in social or family settings for an extended period. They prefer to keep to themselves or latch onto one individual to reduce their anxiety in social situations. In many cases, they do not know what to talk about or fear saying something embarrassing.

Emotionally disconnected adults race through life with their heads down and, in so doing, are unable to observe what's going on around them. Their Inner Child wants to maintain a low profile in hopes of not being noticed – *"don't call on me!"*

Apart from anger, sadness, happiness, and fear, these inner children find it challenging to identify and express their core emotions. They also struggle to connect with the feelings of others around them. This leads others to think of them as aloof and distant. The real problem is they are just not very observant of their surroundings and others. And that is a common complaint from loved ones – *"he's in the room, but he may as well be miles away."*

As teens, these kids may resort to self-harm activities such as cutting, scratching, or hair pulling. They use these self-destructive activities to feel something, even if those feelings result in intense pain and suffering. It's an unfortunate situation.

The Need for Control Child

If you like chaos, raise your hand. No takers, huh? Most people do not like being surrounded by turmoil and drama. However, for some young children, that is precisely the environment they were raised in. Their homes were habitats of disorder and, in some cases, mayhem.

Some were emotionally, mentally, physically, or sexually abused. Others suffered from neglect. Whatever the conditions they faced, the backdrop was bedlam. And through all the pain and suffering these young kids endured, they understood one critical point – they lacked the power to change things. As a result, they were stuck like animals in a cage, having to endure whatever came their way. Welcome to the jungle.

"I felt completely powerless as a child," said Noah, who was subjected to a traumatic childhood and has struggled with an eating disorder his entire adult life. *"Mom and dad constantly fought, and I was beaten regularly at school. Food was the solution for me. I finally had control of something. It was my thing – unfortunately."*

These individuals have all grown up to be driven by their inner children, who are control freaks. Why? Because as the past demonstrated, when a situation is out of control, they suffer harmful consequences.

These inner children believe they are preventing bad things from occurring by taking control of circumstances. Of course, that is the furthest thing from the truth. Their controlling nature often increases anxiety for both themselves and those around them. And in any circumstances where they cannot obtain control, they turn to their addiction for comfort and escape.

The Entitled-Spiteful Child

It is not unusual for toddlers to *"want what they want."* Humanity's natural selfishness is displayed in children's youthfulness and innocence. Fortunately, the vast majority of us grow out of this mindset and learn to be patient, understanding, and how to share.

However, for children who are made to feel devalued, a sense of entitlement can develop as they hold on to past resentments and cynicism. These kids were given the message that their desires and needs did not matter, leading to anger and bitterness. As adults, when similar emotional pain erupts, causing the Inner Child to scream, *"my needs don't matter,"* the entitlement wheel starts in motion. It is important to note, this child does not feel entitled because he/she feels they are better than others. Instead, it is because they were never made to feel valued. Therefore, they react because they believe *"life is not fair."*

When the Inner Child perceives things are going wrong (even if they may not be), the attitude is to seek pleasure-enhancing activities. And it does not matter if the actions are destructive because the mindset of *"I deserve this"* is more powerful than any sense of right and wrong. But that is where spitefulness can kick in and create chaos. Our inner children learn to "treat" their sense of entitlement through addiction.

The Inferior-Weak Child

The emotional suffering and destruction caused by callous behavior, such as bullying, cannot be emphasised enough. For many kids, being tormented by mean-spirited children and sometimes adults leads to low self-esteem and a self of worthlessness. In the worst cases, it can result in suicide. Over time, if this browbeating continues, some individuals will be conditioned to believe they are weak and inferior. Again, this behavior can come at the hands of parents, siblings, peers, or other authority figures. The source does not matter; it is the outcome of such treatment that results in a child feeling subjacent to others and leading to severe consequences as an adult.

To cope with her inferiority complex, Lizzie, who grappled with a drug and alcohol addiction, hid behind a mask of false confidence. *"I had a massive ego but low self-esteem. I would act like the comedian in the room, but I was dying on the inside."*

There was no safe haven as children, and they constantly lived feeling anxious about what tomorrow would bring. These inner children live in a dangerous world. They are frightened children and always on the lookout for what they perceive as situations that could make them feel weak and inferior.

This is one of the most troubling of the 11 inner children because of the damage it inflicts on these individuals, as they constantly battle feelings of inadequacy and their self-worth continues to erode.

The Stressed Child

Of the 11 inner children, the Stressed Child is an immensely popular choice among clients who have undergone the Inner Child Model. If you were one of these kids raised in a stressful and chaotic environment, you probably learned coping mechanisms (distractions) along the way to block out most of your anxiety. Deploying these means of escape didn't mean the tension was gone; it was just that you learned to avoid dwelling on it.

Although raised in a tumultuous environment, these children probably appeared well-adjusted and happy. But that is only what others saw on the outside. What was beneath the iceberg was relentless worrying.

Over time, you learned to desensitise your anxiousness to the point where you were oblivious to its existence. In fact, children are sometimes so good at hiding their anxiety that they don't realise its intensity.

But the truth of the matter is anxiety is never entirely suppressed. It always leaks out. How? Here are some examples:

- Restlessness
- Awkwardness
- Obsessive-Compulsive Behaviors
- Over-reactivity
- Mood Swings
- Perfectionism
- Social Isolation
- Compulsiveness
- Chronic Complaining of Physical Issues
- Defiant Behaviors
- Depression

These inner children found many ways to distract themselves from emotional anxiety, including imagination, television, the Internet, and reading, to name but a few. But then they stumbled across one of the most effective ways to sidetrack this anxiety – behaviors that ultimately led to addiction. These activities provided a satisfying and fulfilling rush that created a carefree existence – even if only for a short time.

"Crack helped me block out the degrading beatings from my stepfather," recounts Clinton, a 27-year-old musician. *"He would beat me black and blue and lock me up in my room like an animal. I used to sob for hours and wish he was dead. Crack was the answer, as it gave me an escape and oblivion. However, I always came crashing back to earth with a bang."*

Just as it did in childhood, their addiction today serves to soothe anxiety and take away the world's worries. That is until the high is gone, and it is back to reality. Anxiety re-appears, so they rely more heavily on addictive activities to lessen their stress level. And very soon, they are caught in a vicious cycle that heightens their overall stress while adding a liberal dose of shame into the equation.

Where to get the next fix, how to keep the secrets hidden, and the shamefulness of these activities all add to the stress level they initially sought to reduce. What started as a tension reliever has now, insidiously, become an addictive habit.

Early Sexually Stimulated/Sexually Abused Child

When children endure sexual abuse, it changes everything. Their worldviews regarding people, security, trust, and innocence dramatically alter. Various defense mechanisms are created to maintain a semblance of sanity and safety. Unfortunately, in many cases, child sexual abuse is hidden, and these innocent victims keep their pain to themselves.

While statistics vary, studies show only 12 to 30% of child sex abuse cases are reported. Horrifyingly, this means most children who suffer at the hands of sexual predators must learn how to cope alone with the enormous shame and guilt. When children carry the burden of harboring a horrible secret, it is a safe bet they will suffer additional emotional and mental consequences for years to come.

"My brother said if I told anyone, mom and dad would go to jail," recalls Dale, 48, a married father of four, who was sexually abused on numerous occasions by his older brother and had been dealing with problematic sexual behaviors and alcohol-related troubles his entire life. *"I knew it was wrong, but I was too scared to speak out."*

Others in this group were subjected to sexual stimulation early in their lives. This early exposure might have been accidentally stumbling across pornography, or environmental exposure to sex, for example, hearing parents having sex several nights a week through the walls of their adjoining bedrooms.

Early sexual stimulation or being sexually abused can lead individuals to develop irrational beliefs, including the conviction that they are dirty or defective. In these cases, the Inner Child may encourage the individual to punish themselves, which may involve behaviors that lead to addiction.

Spiritually Abused Child

The spiritually abused child grew up in confusing and sometimes emotionally and mentally painful circumstances. Whether it was parents or out-of-control authority figures, they were left feeling guilty about their thoughts, emotions, and behaviors based on unrealistic or false spiritual doctrines and messages.

Often, abusive and unethical treatment is meted out that can negatively affect a child's self-worth and decision-making ability. In these cases, children are often micro-managed and fed messages that lead to feelings of shame and guilt. In more severe cases, as adults, these individuals will go on to suffer from post-traumatic stress disorder, depression, and cognitive dissociation.

Here are some key characteristics explaining the development of the Spiritually Wounded Child.

- Raised in a legalistic, rigid environment driven by religious rules and regulations
- Taught to have an unholy fear of God
- Suffered abuse at the hands of church leaders
- Dealt with self-loathing and perhaps self-harm
- Disconnected from others
- May have poor critical thinking skills and difficulty making decisions

HEADS UP: If this is your story and you have not sought professional help, it is strongly encouraged that you seek assistance to help you process and heal from the horrific childhood wounds you endured. You owe it to yourself.

The Enmeshed Child

These children are raised in environments where they are indoctrinated into believing that meeting a parent's emotional needs is more important than their own emotional well-being. Enmeshment occurs when there is a lack of independence between family members, and the individuals meld together, erasing any trace of distinct boundaries.

Without these boundaries, the environment is highly tense and feels suffocating. Enmeshed children are taught how they should feel and think. There is no autonomy, just the development of a "groupthink" mentality. The home atmosphere is rigid and driven by an overabundance of rules that must be strictly adhered to by family members.

These children feel responsible for managing the emotions, and especially the happiness, of others. This, of course, comes at the expense of their own needs and desires. This stifling environment also leaves children confused about their own identities.

Addiction Creates Runners

So, there you have it – the 11 inner children who impact your addiction. As you can see, there is a level of psychological complexity not fully understood by most individuals dealing with an addiction. But once you have the insight associated with your inner children, you will be prepared to go on a journey of recovery that will lead you far beyond behavioral modification. It will also put you on the pathway to change your negative narratives, allowing you to shift toward a more positive and rewarding way to see yourself.

As you may have noticed, one common theme runs throughout these 11 inner children – all of them are rooted in emotional pain. In many cases, the distress results from events that took place years or even decades ago and have been locked away in our subconscious minds. Being unaware of what we genuinely feel can leave us frustrated as we endeavor to understand *why* we engage in destructive behaviors toward ourselves and others.

The truth is we don't recognise the core emotional triggers that lead us to act out because they are suppressed. Our Inner Child, however, is very much in tune with them. And that is why it is critical to connect deeper with your child and understand the triggers that activate him/her.

With this book and professional help, you can identify the core emotional triggers that cause your Inner Child to have tantrums that push you to escape via addictive behaviors. When you start getting your hands dirty and touching raw nerves that activate your Inner Child, you will discover your emotional pain is more profound and intense than you ever imagined.

But with the insight into what triggers the kid comes the ability to develop an action plan to instruct and soothe him. And in so doing, you can learn to manage your unwanted behaviors.

We who battle addiction are "runners." We struggle to confront the emotional demons experienced in our youth and instead seek to ignore them by indulging in alcohol, drugs, sex, food, etc. By running, we do not need to face negative emotions. Instead, we keep distancing ourselves from the potential pain by engaging in stimulating and distracting activities.

Unfortunately, there is a high price for this inability to face the feelings that haunt us. By not knowing how to deal with our emotional brokenness, we suffer horrendous consequences such as fractured relationships, financial hardships, health issues, loss of employment, and legal difficulties, to name but a few. It is a sad situation that leaves many of us feeling hopeless.

Why Bother?

You are probably asking yourself, *"why should understanding the reason(s) I struggle with addiction be part of my recovery."* Good question. The answer is the reason(s) you uncover allow you to get to the root of your destructive behavior without understanding *why* you continue to use your addiction to distract from your underlying emotional distress and limit your ability to get to the bedrock of the problem. Defeating an addiction should not be limited to changing behaviors but should involve changing how you feel about yourself.

A key in this transformation process is understanding *why* you turn to addictive substances and behaviors in the first place. And to accomplish that, you need to become aware and involved with your Inner Child.

EXTREMELY IMPORTANT INFORMATION

Let's stop here to once again reinforce the point that these 11 inner children are **NOT** excuses for your addiction. Instead, these should serve as insights to help you identify and deal with hidden emotional pain, that you are medicating by using addictive substances and behaviors as a distraction and/or stimulant. You should in no way hide behind these rationales as justification for your misguided behaviors. Instead, these reasons should be utilised as tools in your recovery process to help provide much-needed self-reflection about **why** you engage in destructive behaviors.

Getting Started

The contents of this book will challenge you in ways you have never been challenged before. We will go beyond your addiction and explore the emotional pain and scars that people and events left upon you as a child and/or teenager. We will drill deep to uncover what is at the core of your addiction and discover your Inner Child's core emotional triggers.

We're not going to kid you. This process can be extremely painful, but in the end, you will experience a sense of relief and freedom you have never felt. You will have the insights to shield yourself against temptation, help you comfort your Inner Child, and ultimately manage your addiction.

Moving forward, we will review the 11 children in more depth. Carefully analysing each one will most likely uncover 3–5 you believe drive your destructive behaviors. It is rare to select only one child, and most choose 3–5 that thoroughly explain their addiction. Some have picked all 11. After carefully reviewing the list, put them in order of priority based on which ones you associate with most.

Based on this brief introduction, you probably have already started concluding the children related to your addiction. But be patient with this process. As you review each Inner Child in more depth, you will develop additional self-awareness and insights that may change or add to your initial selections.

The key is to reflect on each of these children and not rush through the process. You want to walk away with the clarity that will enable you to create an effective game plan to combat your addiction moving forward. So, let's begin this new and exciting journey.

Workbook

1   Which Inner Children did you **resonate** with?

Bored Child ☐   Unnoticed Child ☐   Unaffirmed Child ☐
Emotionally Void Child ☐   Need for Control Child ☐   Stressed Child ☐
Entitled/Spiteful Child ☐   Inferior/Weak Child ☐   Enmeshed Child ☐
Early Sexually Stimulated/
   Abused Child ☐
Spiritually Wounded Child ☐

2   Take a moment to consider **why** you selected each of these children. What did you see in these children and their experiences that reminded you of when you were growing up? Be as detailed as possible.

_____
_____
_____
_____
_____

3   If you selected more than three children, **list them**, starting with "A" being the strongest.

A .
B .
C .
D .
E .
F .

4   What made you select the order of these children? What **stands out** most in the descriptions you read?

_____
_____
_____
_____
_____

One common theme for these children is their inability to sit with emotional distress. Instead, they become runners, seeking to escape their discomfort by using addictive substances and behaviors. But running from your emotional pain or discomfort is not a solution. Instead, you must learn to endure the pain and begin the healing process.

5   Can you relate to the idea of **running away from emotional distress** by escaping into your addiction?

Yes ☐   No ☐   Not sure ☐

6 If you answered yes to question 5, describe why your addiction is a **good distraction** for the emotional distress you suffer.

_____

_____

_____

_____

_____

7 Although it's early in our studies, have you been able to think of any potential **Core Emotional Triggers** that activate your Inner Child?

Yes ☐   No ☐

8 If yes, what do you think they are?

_____

_____

_____

_____

_____

These are not excuses for our troubling and hurtful behaviors. Instead, they are rationales to help us understand "why" we acted the way we did.

Inner Child Exercise

Below, using your **non-dominant hand**, draw a picture of your Inner Child. Close your eyes and visualise their posture, height, and the expression on your child's face. Can you capture what the child is feeling? Then answer the questions under the drawing.

My Inner Child Drawing

What is the child's name? _____

How old is the Child?_____

What is the child feeling? _____

What help does the child need from me?

_____

_____

_____

_____

_____

Well done! Now **comment** below: what are two key points you found most interesting in this chapter? Be as specific as possible in your answers.

_____

_____

_____

_____

_____

Chapter 4

The Bored Child

Jack grew up a lonely child who confronted boredom daily. But as a teen and later an adult, Jack found an antidote to his colorless life that kept him charged up and filled with stimulation. Sex.

He presented in therapy with an addiction to pornography, webcams, and chat rooms – all forms of anonymous sex that did not require personal interaction. And that is the way Jack liked it (Figure 4.1).

He was raised by his grandmother shortly after he was born. His father left home before his birth, and his mother developed post-natal depression and was incapable of caring for him. His grandmother became the only mother he ever knew.

Jack's grandmother, while not abusive, was detached and stoic. She provided the basic care he required but no more. There was very little conversation in the house, and he can recall little positive interaction with her.

"I spent most of my childhood stuck in my head," he recalled. *"I had no friends, my father had left, my mother was nowhere to be found, and my grandmother rarely interacted with me. I felt like an outcast.*

"So, I found myself in my bedroom most of the time," said Jack, a 30-year-old postal worker who had never been married. *"I had lots of electronics starting at an early age, so those kept me occupied. But there was little human interaction."*

Distractions and More Distractions

For children like Jack, engaging in healthy relationships with others was limited or non-existent, leaving them to rely on their imaginations to generate excitement. However, with little engagement, and few experiences and interactions with others, their imaginations can become stagnant.

To combat loneliness, some kids employ the first behavior that can subsequently lead to addiction as they become glued to the television, the Internet, video games, or overeating. These activities provide substantial stimulation and help distract from the mental and emotional distress of feeling bored and isolated.

"When I was 7, I started playing video games for hours on end," Jack continued. *"This was the most stimulation I had ever experienced, and it was great. I felt alive, and I did not feel bored anymore. Video games became my go-to in dealing with being bored."*

However, these activities cannot replace healthy, interactive relationships, which we all desire and need, whether consciously or subconsciously. And eventually, over time, these forms of entertainment become tiring, so something more powerful is needed to distract from boredom. This is especially true as life becomes more difficult for a child to manage.

For Jack, at school, things were worse than at home. He was bullied daily, which forced

DOI: 10.4324/9781003406013-4

Figure 4.1

him to retreat further into his shell. The only escape for this young boy was his video games, but even they were starting to lose the ability to distract him from thinking about what awaited him on the playground. But not to worry, Jack was about to uncover a new stimulant that would be extremely powerful in helping him block out his sad world.

"I was around 12 when I came across pornography online," he said as his voice lowered in shame. *"It soon became the highlight of my day. After surviving another day of terror at school, I headed straight to my room and into my virtual world of porn. Grandma never checked on me, and I knew what time dinner was and would come out, eat and then retreat for more porn.*

"Watching porn was mesmerizing," he said. *"The women were beautiful, and I know this sounds crazy, but sometimes I thought they were looking at me and would be interested in me. When I was watching porn, the rest of my life did not exist."*

Your Inner Child Runs the Show

The Inner Child of those who grew up with little positive stimulation is emotionally triggered today when events leave them feeling rejected, abandoned, lonely, fearful, or bored, to name a few. But since the Inner Child works in your subconscious, you are often unaware when the kid is triggered. When the child is activated, you experience increased anxiety or discomfort. Refusing to experience the pain, you seek comfort in behaviors that soothe your distress.

"So many emotions triggered me that it was difficult sometimes to get through the day without wanting to go back to drinking," said Dolores, a 52-year-old librarian who did

therapy with the Inner Child Model for two years and had been sober for five. *"After my divorce eight years ago, I would wake up feeling lonely and abandoned, although I know my husband didn't have much choice but to leave me since I could not get my drinking under control.*

"But once I understood these emotions, I was experiencing was not something I could brush aside, but instead I needed to face, my life changed dramatically," she continued. *"I learned to become more attentive to the little girl in me and recognise when she felt alone. It was powerful to learn I could healthily experience my emotions instead of ignoring them."*

Dolores grew up not experiencing much in the way of emotions. As a child, she spent most of her time alone. Living in a rural area with no children her age, a father who was rarely home, and a mother who buried herself in a bottle every day, this young girl was forced to care for herself. She found life to be lonely and boring.

"Books were my friend growing up; I could get lost in reading for hours," she recalled. *"It took away the pain of having nothing to do but chores and having no one to talk with. Even at school, I withdrew from everyone because I felt I could not relate to things they were interested in or experienced. Books saved my life."*

Key Characteristics of the Bored Child

What are some key characteristics that explain the development of the Bored Child?

- Live in a low-key, quiet existence as children and teenagers
- No, or limited, emotional engagement with others
- Often feel isolated and alone
- Learn to entertain themselves (live in fantasy a great deal)
- Seek out adrenaline-based activities that fuel addictive behaviors
- May engage in self-mutilation activities such as cutting, hair pulling, burning self to feel something
- Become laser-focused on new-found outlets for stimulation
- As adults, programmed to fill any quiet moments with the quest to obtain a chemical rush delivered by addictive pursuits

How It Went Wrong

There are numerous reasons why children grow up in an emotionally empty or low-key environment that provides little positive stimulation. Some parents ignore the emotional needs of their children. These individuals are too focused on their own issues and desires instead of looking outward and focusing on their sons and daughters.

They continue living life as they did before they had children. Often, they assume if a child is not complaining, everything is ok. The kid is content and does not need anything from them. But these parents could not be more wrong. What this amounts to is neglect.

"Starting at the age of 7, my parents assumed I could do everything on my own and that I did not need their help," said Roger, 37, who deals with a gambling addiction that cost him everything. *"Their passion was their restaurant and catering business which they loved far more than my older brother or me.*

"We were left alone all hours of the day and night," he recalled. *"We were true latch-key kids. Mom would leave us dinners that we would heat, but we did the rest. Laundry, cleaning, getting ready for school, making our lunches, everything.*

"But the worst part was no supervision," he continued. *"We watched R-rated movies, surfed the internet, and saw things we should have never seen. You would think this would be a kid's dream, no one bugging him. But not for me. I was bored with all of it. What I wanted more than anything was time with my mom and dad.*

"When I was in my mid-teens, I came across online gambling games," he continued. *"I played free games until I went to college and got a job. I never thought playing for cash was so much more exciting than those free games. As I got older and married, my desire for gambling grew, and so did my losses."*

The Distracted Parent

Then there are the distracted parents. These are often well-meaning people, but they are consumed by pressing issues that leave them with little bandwidth for these inner children. In some cases, they are dealing with a special needs or rebellious child who requires tremendous amounts of attention.

Sometimes, finances or employment serve as the focal point for their attention. These parents may deal with personal problems, such as chronic illnesses, mental health disorders, addiction, or depression. Whatever the scenario, there are children left behind to fend for themselves.

Georgia always remembered her mother being ill. Dealing with a severe heart condition, her mom required much bed rest. Her father divorced her mom when Georgia was four because he could not deal with his wife's chronic condition. To prevent her from worrying about her daughter's whereabouts, Georgia's mother did not allow her to leave the house and home-schooled the girl despite spending little time checking on her progress.

"It was like being a prisoner in my own home," said Georgia, who left home when she turned 18 to live with a guy she met on the Internet. He would introduce her to a drug-filled lifestyle, later forcing her into prostitution to support their drug habit. *"I was so bored as a child and teen. There was only so much television you could watch or music you could listen to. I started cutting myself around the age of 14 so that I could feel something. And when I was 18, I ran out of that house as fast I could, leaving it all behind, including my mother."*

Boredom and isolation made a young woman desperate for emotional and mental stimulation, which she received from Hank, whom she met in a chatroom three months before her 18th birthday.

"The words he wrote in his chats were so loving and caring. I felt as though he knew me and what I needed," she explained as a faint smile appeared on her face. *"And he did. But he used it to manipulate me. The day after I moved in with him and several of his friends, he stuck a needle into my arm, which was the beginning of my new path to hell."*

"He was a bad guy, and I'm lucky I was able to escape him, but he caused a lot of damage," she said as tears rolled down her face. *"But then, so did my mother and father. I never saw my father again after he left the house. No one cared, or at least they did not show it. I am sure there were other ways my mom could have raised me that would have allowed me to interact with others. Instead, she took away my life the same way her life had been taken from her."*

The Emotionally Stunted Family

Isolation bond boredom are the norms for those raised in an environment that offers little to encourage family members to share emotions. Even when surrounded by people, these children feel isolated and alone due to the lack of personal connection and nurturing.

Instead, they are left unchallenged to grow and develop the emotional skills required to be a healthy adult.

Growing up, these kids learned that expressing emotions was not acceptable or safe. So, instead, they kept to themselves and spent far too much time in fantasy and daydreaming. They developed the unhealthy habit of "staying in their heads."

"I always wondered what was wrong with me," said Carl, who, at 49, has dealt with sexual addiction for nearly three decades. *"In my entire life, I have never had any real passions. There have been moments of happiness here and here, but I feel as though I am simply walking through life most of the time. My relationships lack passion. My work lacks passion. There is no passion, period. While I don't want to kill myself, I wouldn't be sad if it was my time to go."*

Although he does not consider it, sex has been Carl's passion. It is a driving force in his life, and he turns to it several times a day to stimulate what he perceives to be a mundane life.

"Whenever I am bored – which is too frequently – I start searching the escort ads," said Carl. *"I always tell myself I am just going to look, but it rarely ends there, and I act out. When I go through the ads, it's like I am hunting, and that's sometimes more exciting than the sexual experience itself."*

A life lacking stimulation, which started as a child when he was forbidden to share his emotions, continues to lead Carl to seek continuous mental and emotional jump-starts. He uses sex to create sparks he knows will generate an emotional inferno of bliss that cannot be achieved by any other means. Sexual stimulation – whether real or merely fantasy – is the antidote to pushing aside boredom and lack of purpose that has haunted him all his life.

Jack Continued

So let's return to the story of Jack, who was raised by his distant grandmother and became addicted to pornography. Entrapped in a life of boredom may have been depressing for him as a child and teen, but its continuation into his adult life would have crippling consequences.

"And when I was 15, I found chatrooms, and the rush became more intense. People on here wanted to interact with me. I could pretend to be whoever I wanted, so I developed a persona and called myself Jackie telling people I was 18. The experience was exhilarating."

As time went on, his porn usage escalated and took a dark turn. *"At the start, it was just vanilla porn, but I needed more stimulation to combat the boredom as time progressed. I started watching genres that went against my values and morals and developed a fetish.*

Gradually, as Jack became desensitised to the porn he was watching, he began seeking illegal content to give himself the shock and stimulation his mind had now required. *"I was completely out of control; it was as if I was possessed,"* he said. *"It completely went against who I was as a person. I felt sickened and ashamed of the things I was watching. Then one day, the police were at my door."*

Jack had been accessing underage images, and he was arrested and convicted. He was placed on the sex offenders register for 15 years.

After his conviction, he entered treatment and, finally, could see how his addiction had assumed the role of his parents, teaching him about sex, love, and connection. But, of course, everything he learned was the opposite of what he needed. Over time, as he worked on healing from his attachment wounds, he gained more confidence to take chances and connect with others,

"It has been a long road, and it's not over, but now I have friends, a career, and have even reconnected with my mother," he said. *"I no longer spend time online trying to fill the*

emptiness and boredom. I can see how something I thought was helping me was scarring me. I am so grateful I have left that life behind. I am no longer 'Jackie.' I am free."

Kid Talk

Along with helping your Inner Child process painful emotional triggers, how else can you comfort this child? Start by teaching the child that boredom is a **choice**. By adjusting your mindset, you can seek creative and healthy ways to keep the mind active.

This kid needs to be encouraged to explore life and take risks by seeking new, healthy experiences. The bored child desires to participate in exciting activities that provide positive stimulation. What these activities are will depend upon your interests. Now we hear you saying, *"but I don't have any interests."* Perhaps. But that becomes part of your journey – to seek out potential activities that will generate new-found passions in your life.

Stuck for ideas? Well, understand that *"Google is your friend."* Use it to generate ideas that can bring positive excitement into your life. For example, by Googling "what bored adults can do," you will find numerous articles such as *"96 Things to Do When You're Bored."*

Again, it is about becoming curious and exploring potential activities to overcome boredom. Hopefully, you will create a healthy list of activities to partake in when feelings of boredom creep in.

But none of this will work if you do not develop a new mindset about life. Do you want to live or just exist? That will be the driving factor to determine whether you can overcome a boring life or not.

Core Emotional Triggers

The chart below provides a list of core emotional triggers that can activate the Inner Child who grew up bored and isolated. If boredom is one of your reasons **why**, take time to review this list of emotions. Which ones make you feel uncomfortable? Those are your core emotional triggers as they relate to the bored child.

Only select the troublesome ones and start developing your Core Emotional Triggers list. You will do this exercise for each of the inner children as we move forward.

Why is this important? Because you act out when your Inner Child is activated. If you realise the child is triggered, you can work to soothe the kid instead of being driven to escape into addictive activities.

Core Emotional Triggers of the Bored Child

This is only a partial list and you may identify additional triggers. Remember, these emotions occur based on the way your Inner Child perceives a current situation. However, the kid's perception of events may be inaccurate.

Life Is Boring	I'm Alone
I'm Jealous	I Feel Empty
I'm a Dull Person	Life Has No Purpose
I Don't Care	I'm Invisible

EXTREMELY IMPORTANT INFORMATION

We just reviewed scenarios of home environments that lacked stimulation. Please note, this is not a complete list of examples. As you ponder your childhood you may find you experienced different circumstances that led to a low-key existence. That's ok. Space doesn't permit us to write about every potential scenario that could negatively impact us as children.

And there are no cookie-cutter answers to determining what led to your addictive behavior. That is true for each of the 11 children outlined in this book.

Challenge yourself to explore more deeply what you experienced in your youth and the impact it had on your Inner Child. The more you explore and self-reflect, the more conclusive your answer to the *why* question will become.

Workbook

1   Do you **resonate** with the Bored Child?

Yes ☐   No ☐

2   If yes, why do you **resonate** with this child? What conditions did you grow up in that left you bored and perhaps alone? Write your story. Be as specific as possible.

_____

_____

_____

_____

_____

3   Do you think **boredom** is a factor that has driven you to engage in addictive behaviors?

Yes ☐   No ☐   Not sure ☐

4   If you answered yes to question 3, why do you **believe** boredom is a factor?

_____

_____

_____

_____

_____

5   Can you **recall** when you first experienced an intense adrenaline rush as a child or teen? If so, what was it?

_____

_____

_____

_____

_____

Boredom can be dangerous. It makes us restless and leads to a hunt for stimulation and adrenaline. Many who struggle with addiction succumb to boredom because they do not have enough interests and passions. That needs to change as you move through recovery.

6   Which Core Emotional **Triggers** do you experience when you face boredom and loneliness?

Life is boring ☐   I'm alone ☐   I'm invisible ☐
I'm jealous ☐   I feel empty ☐   Life has no purpose ☐
I feel restless ☐   Other: _____

7 Take each trigger at a time and **explain** why you selected it and how it originated. Again, write your story and be as specific as possible.

_____

_____

_____

_____

_____

8 How can you healthily respond to these triggers? What **ideas** do you have for doing this?

_____

_____

_____

_____

_____

9 What are some potential **hobbies** or interests you may want to explore? Start brainstorming here.

_____

_____

_____

_____

_____

10 Well done! Now **comment** below: what are two key points you learned in this chapter? Be as specific as possible in your answers.

_____

_____

_____

_____

_____

Chapter 5

The Unaffirmed Child

The old saying about sticks and stones is flawed and stupid. As you know, words can be just as destructive, or even more so, than a physical attack. And while damaging words thrown in the direction of an adult can be painful, those words hurled at a child can cause confusion and permanent psychological harm (Figure 5.1).

A child should expect unconditional love and acceptance, which starts in the arms of a nurturing mother and father. This positive affirmation, in turn, develops strong and healthy self-esteem.

But in many cases, kids do not receive the necessary affirmation needed to develop that healthy self-worth. And sometimes, they receive the opposite – extensive criticism – which leads to troubling consequences.

But there are also cases where parents express their disapproval of a child, sometimes directly and sometimes indirectly. This often occurs when a parent has expectations of a child the kid simply cannot meet. In many cases, love is conditional and based on the child's performance. Good performances are praised and rewarded, while poor performances often result in silent disappointment. That was Debra's experience when she went from being the center of attention to an afterthought in a split second.

Debra, 51, is married with three children. She came to counseling to deal with a gambling and cocaine addiction. Raised in an affluent family where academic and athletic achievements came naturally to all family members, Debra was no exception.

"It's all we ever heard as kids – make sure you do well at school and pick a sport you are good at," Debra said during her initial session. She was a keen long-distance runner, excelling at regional and national levels.

"My dream growing up was to run in the Olympics and win a medal. Every day I would fantasise about standing on the podium and winning gold," she continued. *"And my parents were my biggest cheerleaders. I thought what they were displaying was love but what they were cheering was finding glory through my success."*

Her World Changes

Everything was going to plan for Debra as she worked with Olympic trainers to hone her skills. Yes, it was all going great until that split-second occurred.

"I was 14 and was training for a spot on the national team when I slipped and broke my ankle in three places," she said in a downcast voice. *"That was the end of my sports dreams. But I didn't know at the time. It also was the end of receiving my parents' love and attention."*

Specialists told Debra that she would no longer be able to compete on the same level, and that was the end of her sports career.

DOI: 10.4324/9781003406013-5

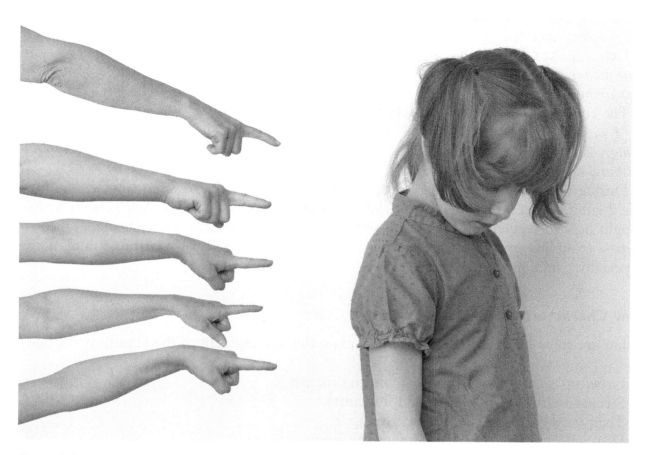

Figure 5.1

"It felt like my stomach had been ripped out – the despair I felt was excruciating," she recalled. *"But what I remembered more was the reaction of my parents. They didn't say much of anything to me except 'it will be ok.' My father could barely look at me. I felt ashamed."*

As she got older, it was heartbreaking for Debra to watch her two siblings achieve major accomplishments in the sporting world.

"Don't get me wrong, I was happy for my brothers, but I was also envious of the praise and recognition they were receiving from my parent while mine was gone," Debra said. *"They didn't criticise me, instead they just displayed their disappointment by having nothing positive to say to me. I was left alone to deal with my pain. I was no one."*

After college, Debra went to law school, where she did well but did not pass the bar exam.

"After failing my law exam, I decided I had had enough. I needed oblivion, so hit the bottle," she recalled. *"I felt inferior and a let-down to my family. My family did not acknowledge my accomplishments in law school, only that I did not pass the exam. I was so done with them."*

Life Gets Darker

Debra descended into a life of drinking, drugs, and trips to the casino. After marrying, having children, and a period of sobriety, Debra set up a business that proved hugely successful. This coincided with the advent of online casinos and gambling websites.

"I remember being at work one day when a deep sadness overcame me that I couldn't pinpoint," Debra said. *"I was browsing the internet and came across an online casino. It offered $25 to register – I signed up. This was the beginning of the end for me. I gambled at*

work and stayed up all night after everyone had gone to bed. I lost $250k over six months, and the cocaine came back with a vengeance to fill this pain and blank out the consequences."

Debra spoke of a time she lost $100k in one evening. *"It was like a blur – it didn't feel like real money. I sat downstairs with a bottle of wine, lines of cocaine, and my laptop screen displaying a virtual roulette table. My family slept upstairs as I lost myself in my addiction."*

The consequences proved devastating for her.

"I was finally found out when the company accounts were checked. I nearly lost everything," she recalled as she lowered her head in sadness as she spoke. *"I confessed all to my husband and entered treatment."*

During therapy, Debra could see how failing the bar exam triggered similar emotions she'd felt after her injury and the lack of acceptance from her parents. Also, Debra wasn't taught how to regulate emotions and process painful experiences. Instead, she learned to bypass troubling emotions and situations by distracting herself with various stimulations, especially gambling and coke.

Key Characteristics of the Unaffirmed Child

What are some key characteristics that explain the development of the Unaffirmed Child?

- Grow up receiving little praise or much criticism
- Struggle with low self-worth and insecurity
- Their worldview is "I don't measure up"
- Deal with self-loathing and perhaps self-harm
- Receive ongoing affirmation that is suddenly withdrawn
- Afraid to take chances for fear of failing
- Maybe resentful and defiant, or fade into the background
- Addictive behaviors feed the self-loathing

What Goes Wrong

A constant stream of affirmation is necessary for children to believe they are unconditionally loved and accepted by others. Without experiencing these essential emotional bonds, individuals are destined to struggle in relationships because of their poor self-image.

Kids who receive little in the way of affirmation will believe nothing they do is good enough. They always feel they fall short in their efforts to please others and do not get the opportunity to learn how to feel proud of their achievements. Later as adults, if they succeed in the academic or the professional world, their inner children believe their accomplishments are tainted.

This happened to Debra, who could not recognise achievement in passing all her law classes. Instead, she was too focused on failing the bar exam. It did not occur to her that numerous students fail the first time they take the exam.

Because they receive little praise, these individuals lack confidence; therefore, they may be unwilling to take risks. Their Inner Child will push them to hide in the back of the room and become just another face in the crowd. That is a safe place because no one can discover they're a fraud.

"My worry is one day I will be found out, and they will see me for who I am," said Gregory, who was recovering from alcohol abuse. *"I am always second-guessing myself at work, thinking I missed something. And then I panic and retreat into my office until the end of the day when I can stop at the liquor store and prepare myself for an evening of stress reduction with my alcohol."*

The problem with this scenario is that Gregory is a standout at his chemical engineering job. He has multiple advanced educational degrees and certifications. Some consider him a leader in his field of expertise. But he thinks just the opposite.

His grandfather raised him after his parents were killed in a car accident. His grandfather was a brilliant man and the chief operating officer of a major automobile manufacturer. But unfortunately, grandpa didn't have the same excellence in parenting skills.

Gregory's lack of confidence comes from his grandpa questioning his grandson's academic achievements. Grades were never good enough, and even assignments that resulted in an "A" were questioned and debated if they could have been done better.

The message Gregory took away from all of this was, *"you will never be good enough. You don't know what you're doing."*

For a childlike Gregory, whose accomplishments are challenged or belittled, a blanket of shame drapes over them, and they believe they're flawed. And this shame can have devastating consequences as the child becomes a teenager and then an adult, leading them to take several paths to escape the negative emotions lurking beneath the surface.

1 First, some children become angry, resentful, and defiant adults and find it difficult to experience joy and pleasure in anything or anyone. Their shame leaks out in anger, thus allowing them to hand out constant streams of criticism. Although they feel weak and lack confidence, their inner children have them hiding behind a façade of a bully. The Inner Child is on the offensive, and the goal is to hurt others before being hurt. In this scenario, the destructive cycle they experienced as a child continues.
2 This next adult feels weak and lacks confidence, but instead of hiding behind a façade, their Inner Child simply allows them to fade into the background. Shame leads to withdrawing and not taking any risks. They will struggle to identify and express their emotions. According to a 2018 research study conducted at Binghamton University, State University in New York, children of overly critical parents show fewer emotional facial expressions. *"We know from previous research that people tend to avoid things that make them uncomfortable, anxious, or sad because such feelings are aversive. We also know that children with a critical parent are more likely to use avoidant coping strategies when they are in distress than children without a critical parent,"* said Kiera James, a graduate student of psychology at Binghamton University and lead author of the paper.
3 Some children who deal with chronic criticism become adults who fulfill the negative prophecy drilled into their heads at a young age. Their shame is on full display as they give in to the belief, they are worthless. These adults, who endured ruthless criticism as children, struggle in many aspects of life, including career and relationships, because their inner children continue to believe they're undeserving of happiness or success.

Lee – Mr. Loser

Take the case of Lee, who grew up in a home with a teenage mother, a drug-addicted father, and a younger sister. As you can imagine, Lee's home life was engulfed in chaos and turmoil. His mother, practically a child herself, struggled to focus on caring for her kids. She still wanted to be a carefree young adult and often became bored and restless. Meanwhile, his father struggled to stay employed because of his drug addiction, which led him to be unreliable.

Consequently, finances were always an issue, and the family often lived on government assistance. As children, Lee and his sister faced constant verbal and physical abuse from both parents. And while the physical abuse meted out by his father (especially when his dad was high) was extensive, the verbal abuse Lee endured at the hands of his mother was more memorable and cutting.

"She had no filter," Lee said during our earlier sessions. *"Whatever she was thinking came out of her mouth. She used profanity in every sentence, and the name-calling was relentless. If you didn't know my name, and you were around us, after a while, you would have thought it was 'stupid f–.'*

"I could sense at an early age my mom resented my sister and me," he continued. *"She was too young to have children and had a hard life. I want to forgive her, but I still have night-mares of the awful words she used to describe me."*

Lee started viewing pornography at age 11 when he came across his father's collection and discovered it was a pleasant escape from the anxious home environment.

"He had a pretty extensive collection, and some of it was very hardcore," Lee recalled. *"I was incredibly careful to ensure I didn't get caught sneaking it, although that was difficult since we lived in a trailer and he was often home. But whenever I could get my hands on some, I would go out in the woods and get lost for hours viewing the photos."*

But even with pornography as an outlet to help him withdraw, Lee could not escape his mother's constant berating.

"I remember when I was 11, a friend was visiting, and my mom attempted to show me physical affection, which rarely happened," recounted Lee. *"But thinking she was going to hit me, I jerked away. So, what did she do? She slapped me across the face and called me a piece of s... She screamed at me and told my friend to get the f*** out of her house. I was mortified. I remember spending the night in the woods repeatedly masturbating to get the scene out of my head."*

He continued, *"Although I worked hard to stay out of trouble, I was never good enough for either of them,"* he said with his eyes focused on the floor. *"And although I hated the criticism, it didn't bother me as much as the lack of praise. I tried to please them with my actions but never received a positive word of affirmation. I would bring home a good report card or win an award at school, and no one cared. I was not important. What was important to my mom was non-stop entertainment television and my dad getting his next drug hit. Other than that, nothing else mattered, especially my sister or me."*

Lee's Inner Child

Life for Lee hasn't been pleasant. Divorced three times, he is currently single, and his sexual addiction is still in full swing. Today at the age of 56, Lee frequents strip clubs and solicits prostitutes on average three times a week.

"I'm a loser and always have been," he said during a counseling session. *"My mom was right when she said I would never amount to anything. That is why I haven't gotten married again. I know I would mess up the next one too."*

Lee's Inner Child is full of self-loathing. The constant berating suffered as a child and the lack of affirming words have left the kid depressed and defeated. He is a continuous recording that plays in the back of Lee's mind, filling his head with relentless negative narratives.

Lee's Inner Child is triggered by events that make him feel inadequate or worthless, therefore, the kid has no hope, so instead seeks temporary relief from the emotional pain by engaging in highly stimulating and risky sexual activities.

He does not care if he ends up with a sexually transmitted disease or is robbed during a session with a hooker. In his mind, he would deserve it. So what if he blows his entire pay-check on strippers and continues to make his dire financial situation bleaker? He doesn't care.

These individuals desire real intimacy, but to make that commitment is frightening. Their inner children recall being criticised and rejected, and they fear reliving the painful experiences of childhood. Therefore, reaching out and creating authentic relationships – even with their spouse – is scary because they may not respond positively to their invitation. It is easier to be present than to engage.

Kid Talk

The Inner Child who struggles to feel affirmed will need to process many painful moments as you work with him. The key is to listen and understand the depth of the pain and the negative narratives the child believes in. This kid will struggle to believe what you're telling him. For so long, the kid has dwelled on a laundry list of negative beliefs that will be challenging to overcome.

- You need a great deal of patience with this child, but you also must be very firm and direct. Do not allow him/her to trap you into staying in a negative place when you sit with emotional discomfort/pain. Instead, you need to transition from grieving past traumas and painful memories and shift to examining your current situation through the lens of truth. This requires using your "wise mind" instead of the child's emotional thinking. You will learn more about this in Chapter 14.
- Just like the child who craves attention, you need to praise and encourage this kid. Point out victories you achieve during recovery and credit him for working with you to gain success. You are attempting to shut down or quiet your negative-thinking neural pathways and open new ones that focus on positive and affirming messages. Begin to think of you and your Inner Child as teammates.

Helping the Inner Child who struggles with a lack of affirmation is not a short-term process – in fact, overcoming any of these reasons "why" takes dedication, commitment, and time. But a child who received little affirmation and much criticism has been set up for failure as an adult. Over the years, his self-worth has taken an enormous hit, and rebuilding his confidence can be challenging. Not impossible. Challenging.

Core Emotional Triggers of the Unaffirmed Inner Child

This is only a partial list and you may identify additional triggers. Remember, these emotions occur based on the way your Inner Child perceives a current situation. However, the kid's perception of events may be inaccurate.

I'm a Disappointment	I'm a Failure
I Feel Incompetent	I'm Not Lovable
I'm Stupid	I'm a Mistake
I Feel Insulted	I Feel Inferior
I'm a Loser	I Feel Unloved

Workbook

1 Do you **resonate** with the Unaffirmed Child?

   Yes ☐   No ☐

2 Which of these did you **experience** most growing up?

   A Criticism ☐
   B Lack of affirmation ☐
   C Both ☐

3 What did that **look like**? What conditions did you grow up in that left you feeling unaffirmed and unvalued? Did this occur at home, in school, with peers, or with others? Write your story. Be as specific as you can.

   _____
   _____
   _____
   _____
   _____

4 Do you think being **unaffirmed** is a factor that has driven you to engage in addictive behaviors?

   Yes ☐   No ☐   Not sure ☐

5 If you answered yes to question 4, why do you **believe** this is a factor?

   _____
   _____
   _____
   _____

   Just as children need to feel they belong; they also require positive affirmation to create strong self-worth. Unfortunately, not all children receive this necessary praise and recognition; conversely, they receive a great deal of harsh criticism. If that occurred to you, it breaks our hearts. However, understand you are loved by people in your life who care.

6 Which of these Core Emotional Triggers **resonate** with you?

I am a failure ☐   I am a disappointment ☐   I feel incompetent ☐
I am not lovable ☐   I am stupid ☐   I am a mistake ☐
I feel insulted ☐   I feel inferior ☐   Other: _____

7 Taking each trigger **explain** why you selected it and how it **originated**. Again, write your story and be as specific as possible.

_____
_____
_____
_____
_____
_____

8 How can you healthily respond to these triggers? What **ideas** do you have for doing this?

_____
_____
_____
_____
_____

9 Would you say, as an adult, that you are **hypersensitive** to criticism?

Yes ☐   No ☐

10 How would you react to perceived criticism if you answered yes to question 9? Explain your actions, thoughts, and emotions at the time.

_____
_____
_____
_____
_____

11   Well done! Now **comment** below: what two key points stood out most in this chapter?
     Be as specific as possible in your answers.

     _____

     _____

     _____

     _____

     _____

Chapter 6

The Unnoticed Child

Paul entered therapy to manage his addiction to opiates and alcohol. He would dry up and stay clean for months, only to succumb and undergo another shameful relapse. At 37, married with one child, his wife and family were running out of bandwidth to cope with his inability to stay sober (Figure 6.1).

"I find it difficult to abstain for long periods," he said, occasionally chewing on his fingernails to relieve his anxiety. *"I am not sure what happens. I feel very confident regarding my recovery, but then I can sense my mood shifting over days, and shortly after that, I'm using again."*

When asked to describe this mood change he experienced before a relapse, all Paul could point to was an overwhelming sense of feeling alone. The mood he experienced started to make more sense as Paul outlined his story during his counseling sessions.

He painted the picture of a young boy who spent much of his time trying to fade into the background and avoid being noticed because he constantly lived in fear and anxiety. He was bullied throughout his school years and turned to food to self-soothe, which led to him being overweight.

"I would go to school, suffer all day, then run home to gorge on junk food," he explained, admitting that his diet today is still poor, which would explain his being overweight. *"I had no friends and could not figure out why no one liked me. The only conclusion I came to was that people thought I was weird."*

As you can imagine, school was an anxious place for a kid like Paul, who was meek and endured bullying, and this led to him seeking isolation. Over the years, it became so difficult to make friends he stopped trying. Instead, he focused on studying and would escape into the school library to obtain short breaks from the anxiety he experienced during the school day.

But home life wasn't much better for Paul. He explained that his troubling childhood didn't stop in the schoolyard as his parents also ignored him at home. His father was a bitter man who frowned upon his son's meekness and the fact he was overweight. In addition, Paul's mother provided no comfort or relief for the young boy as she was a passive woman who was emotionally unavailable and lost in her world.

Seeking an Escape

"However hard I tried, I couldn't please my dad," he said. *"He constantly put me down and made me believe I was useless at everything. But for the most part, he ignored me.*

"On the other hand, my mother made me feel invisible," he continued. *"She would say a handful of sentences to me each day. And anything she had to say usually revolved around ensuring things were done to keep my father from becoming angry.*

DOI: 10.4324/9781003406013-6

Figure 6.1

"I may be exaggerating, but I truly can't remember one time when my mother sought me out to spend time with me," he recalled, looking as though he was drifting off into space. *"Even if I hurt myself, she would not go out of her way to help me. And now, as an adult, she still acts as though I am invisible when I'm around her."*

Paul's mom and dad divorced when he was ten years old. His dad set up with another woman and started a new family; *"I was devastated – I tried so hard to reconnect with my dad, but my pleas were ignored. And after he got remarried, he replaced me with new kids."*

As he reached his teenage years, and with his father long out of the picture, Paul found solace in a bottle. *"Alcohol became reliable – it did not bully, judge, or ignore me. Instead, it made me feel better and alive. I didn't think about being invisible or rejected by others."*

Along with the alcohol, Paul began to use benzodiazepines, numbing himself to reduce the negative noise in his head and escape his emotional hell.

"By 16, I was drinking daily and using copious amounts of benzos," he recalled. *"My life was empty. I dropped out of school and was unemployed, living at home. It was a depressing time, and the booze didn't help."*

At 19, Paul got sober, obtained his GED, and found work as an appliance salesman. It looked like his life was back on the right track, however, he did nothing to address the negative noise in his head, which was still telling him he was a loser that no one wanted to be around. So three years into his sobriety, the noise finally caught up with him, and he relapsed.

"Despite being sober, I always felt bad about myself," he said. *"I needed to quiet those negative voices, and I knew alcohol and benzos were problematic, so I decided to use opiates to self-medicate. I thought that would be a safe option, and I could still function.*

"At first, it worked," he continued. *"But the negative voices didn't die down, so I took more and more, and before I knew it, I was back to being unable to function. I lost my job, and I was back to square one."*

Inner Child Theory in Action

During a session, Paul spoke of his most recent relapse and the events which led up to it. *"A friend canceled a night out, which I had been looking forward to for weeks. I felt angry, alone, and abandoned."*

Therapist: *"How old did you feel after your friend broke the news that he was canceling?"*

Paul looked quizzically, then pondered before shrugging his shoulders, and said, *"about 9 or 10 years old."*

Therapist: *"Can you recall what was happening during your life at that age may have felt like abandonment?"*

After a few seconds, Paul's face dropped, and he shrank in his seat. *"It's when dad left us,"* he said in a child-like whisper. *"I came downstairs to leave for school, and he had left a note saying he had gone to be with his new family. I will never forget that day."*

By helping Paul identify the core developmental trauma, he could begin sitting with the emotional distress he had avoided for so long. Assisting him to process and assimilate that heartbreaking experience would enable him to diminish the pain when feelings of abandonment are triggered within him and his Inner Child.

With his new coping strategy and tools, Paul no longer needs to escape the emotional discomfort he feels. Instead, he can confidently face his fear of abandonment and make healthier decisions when triggered.

Why Is Attention Important?

Who does not like attention? As a kid, the thought of grandma reaching out to give us a big hug and pinching our cheeks was warming, especially if she had a $10 bill in her hand. Attention is part of the human need to belong. It soothes the soul to know others long to spend time with you.

But being popular and in demand was something other people experienced – not you. And with that came the belief people were not interested. Not being pursued, you sat on the sidelines, waiting for someone to look your way. But it rarely or never happened.

Growing up, kids like Paul never felt they belonged. They were outcasts and had to chase friends and family members. But rarely did they catch anyone.

In an article in *Psychology Today* magazine, Dr. Robert Mauer points out that when a child struggles to feel desired, the pain never entirely disappears.

"We take for granted that children require attention," he writes. *"Many weary parents come home at night, digging deep inside to find the energy they aren't sure they have to give their little ones the affection they require. But what happens to this need as we grow and become adults? The answer: Nothing changes. The basic human need for attention remains, although sadly, most adults ignore this in themselves and others."*

Key Characteristics of the Unnoticed Child

What are some key characteristics that explain the development of the Unnoticed Child?

- Feel they never belong, rarely chased
- Parents are distracted (own issues or of another child)

- Believe no one cares
- See themselves as different in a bad way
- May become a perfectionist (to earn attention)
- May suffer from low-grade depression

Katelyn's Inner Child

Katelyn was the only child of a single mom raised in a tough city neighborhood. Her mother worked two jobs to make ends meet, often leaving Katelyn alone. When her mother did get home from work, she usually collapsed in bed, exhausted.

Because of the dangers that lurked in her neighborhood, Katelyn was forbidden to go outside on her own. She homeschooled herself and spent the rest of her time in front of the television or fantasizing about living life.

"I thought about my circumstances growing up, and I believe that is what solitary confinement must be like," said the 29-year-old administrative assistant, who now spends her off hours sitting in bars and being picked up by strange men and women. *"I find it difficult to go back to my apartment after work. The thought of being alone and unnoticed is so frightening."*

The fear of being alone that Katelyn experiences comes from her Inner Child, who has grown weary of solitary confinement. Her kid wants to be out and about among people and is willing to engage in reckless sexual activities to avoid feeling invisible. Some of the core emotional triggers that activate Katelyn's Inner Child are:

- I feel abandoned
- I've been left behind
- I feel invisible
- I feel unwanted
- I've been ignored
- No one cares

Any event that brings about one of these emotions will cause Katelyn's Inner Child to become highly anxious and run to seek comfort. An event that triggers some of these emotions occurs at the end of each workday when people start saying goodbye to Katelyn. She usually is the last one to leave the office because of the anxiety she experiences when thinking of returning to her empty apartment.

Instead, she heads to a bar after work two or three times a week to calm her nerves with alcohol and seek companionship for the evening. But this coping mechanism comes at a heavy price.

"Because I am fairly intoxicated when I leave a bar with someone, I don't always practice safe sex," she said as she nervously played with her rings. *"I have had several STDs, been beaten and gang raped. But none of that stops me from continuing to put myself out there. I can't battle the fear of being alone."*

The Inner Child Running the Show

Let us look at what goes wrong when Katelyn's Inner Child gets triggered at the end of the day.

Remember, the fear that haunts Katelyn's Inner Child occurred years ago when she was a child and teenager. All those years without connection with others have made her socially awkward and shy. It is only through drinking that she becomes brave enough to open up to others. Even her co-workers describe her as quiet and uninterested in social interaction.

> Workday Ends and Her Inner Child is Fearful of Going Home

> Katelyn Distracts From Her True Emotion "Loneliness" By Going to a Bar

Today as an adult, Katelyn does have healthier options she could choose to avoid loneliness, however, being emotionally undeveloped stands in her way. Emotionally undeveloped means she was not taught to identify, process, and healthily express her emotions. During the early years of childhood development, her mother did not take the time to provide Katelyn with skills such as attunement, empathy, emotional regulation, processing emotional discomfort, and trust.

Without these essential qualities, Katelyn struggles to make friends and emotionally bond with others. This explains her preference for casual and anonymous sex, which limits the risk of emotional involvement.

Chronic Loneliness

If no one is paying attention to you, one of the most severe consequences is loneliness. Dr. Stacey M. Solomon of the University of Virginia points out that children who endure chronic loneliness can suffer serious consequences.

"Along with increasing a child's vulnerability, chronic childhood loneliness is cause for concern; the consequences potentially have devastating long-term effects," says Dr. Solomon. *"Childhood loneliness has been linked to academic failure, truancy, dropping out of school, and juvenile delinquency as well as mental health problems such as depression, suicide, hostility, alcoholism, poor self-concept, and psychosomatic illnesses."*

For a child to develop strong ego strength, they must receive a positive response to a critical question – *"do I belong?"* We cannot underestimate the importance of knowing others accept, love, and support us. This comes from parents and other family members who provide unconditional love and acceptance. It is found in discovering a secure place and position among peers, where you thrive, knowing you fit in and are not judged.

However, kids feel unwanted and undesired when these conditions don't occur. Like the Bored Child, they experience a sense of loneliness and isolation, even when surrounded by people. They feel left out and question what is wrong with them, that others don't express an interest or concern.

The result for some kids is the development of an unquenchable desire for attention that, in turn, provides self-soothing. To meet this need for attention, they may often participate in elaborate fantasies, positioning themselves as popular, successful, and the envy of others. Some exaggerate their accomplishments or engage in over-the-top bragging and storytelling to get noticed. In some cases, it's not uncommon for these disregarded children to participate in negative behaviors to get attention. As the old saying goes – *"bad attention is better than no attention."*

The Need Goes On

As an adult, the need to be noticed doesn't fade. For example, even if this guy is engaged in a healthy relationship with a partner who shows him attention, it may not be enough to prevent him from being captivated by the new woman in the office who flirts with him.

While he may feel noticed by his wife, his inner kid is fearful the attention will not last. Therefore, the hunt begins to secure a backup plan.

Sean's Inner Child is drawn to people – especially women – who notice him like a moth to a flame. Gravitating toward women who demonstrate interest has become a compulsive reaction for a man who spent too many years not being pursued by people. And it is not unusual for men like Sean to quench their thirst for attention by simultaneously becoming involved in numerous relationships. The attention they receive from multiple women provides an adrenaline rush that keeps them actively seeking more. For these men, sometimes, one is never enough.

Sean's unhealthy need for attention was fueled by the woman who should have demonstrated what real emotional bonding looked like – his mom. His unmet need for attachment to his mother has made it difficult for him to say no to any woman who expressed an interest in him.

"Although I have been with many women since getting married, I have never sought after any of them," he said. *"They would make the first move, which was the most thrilling part. Knowing someone is pursuing me gets my adrenaline soaring."*

The adrenaline Sean refers to is brought on partly by the release of endorphins, protein molecules that flood the brain and generate excitement and elation. Endorphins are likened to morphine in that both occupy the same brain receptors. Now you understand why Sean feels like he is soaring when a woman pursues him – he is feeling no pain.

Kid Talk

The Inner Child who cries out for attention needs to hear from you that he/she is not the problem. Use "wise mind" and rational thinking to show them many circumstances in which they faced rejection resulting from others' insensitivity. Point out to them current relationships where individuals notice and care for them.

Heap words of praise on the kid and let him know he was a good child. Help him to feel unique, valued, and loved. Finally, assure him/her you can manage the situation and will be sure to protect him/her from unsafe people. Help them build trust in you. You probably will be the only person they ever trust.

Core Emotional Triggers of the Unnoticed Inner Child

This is only a partial list and you may identify additional triggers. Remember, these emotions occur based on the way your Inner Child perceives a current situation. However, the kid's perception of events may be inaccurate.

I Feel Rejected	I've Been Dismissed
I Don't Belong	I am Ignored
I am Forgotten	I am Invisible
I am Unseen	I've Been Discarded

Workbook

1 Do you **resonate** with the Unnoticed Child?

Yes ☐   No ☐

2 If yes, why do you **resonate** with this child? What conditions did you grow up in that left you unnoticed and lonely? Did this occur at home, in school, with peers, or with others? Write your story. Be as specific as possible.

_____
_____
_____
_____
_____
_____

3 Do you think being **unnoticed** is a factor that has driven you to engage in addictive behaviors?

Yes ☐   No ☐   Not sure ☐

4 If you answered yes to question 3, why do you **believe** this is a factor?

_____
_____
_____
_____
_____

Feeling you do not belong or are unnoticed can be emotionally crushing for anyone, especially a child. The need to belong is critical to our social development.

5 Which of these Core Emotional Triggers **resonate** with you?

I feel rejected ☐   I've been dismissed ☐   I don't belong ☐
I am ignored ☐   I am forgotten ☐   I am invisible ☐
Other: _____

6 Taking each trigger, **explain** why you selected it and how it originated. Again, write your story and be as specific as possible.

_____
_____
_____
_____
_____

7 How can you healthily respond to these triggers? What **ideas** do you have for doing this?

_____
_____
_____
_____
_____

8 Take time to sit quietly and come up with a few **encouraging words** to share with your Inner Child that will make the little one feel noticed and wanted.

_____
_____
_____
_____
_____

9 Why did you select those words to **encourage** your Inner Child?

_____
_____
_____
_____
_____

10 Well done! Now **comment** below: what two key points stood out most in this chapter? Be as specific as possible in your answers.

_____
_____
_____
_____

Chapter 7

The Emotionally Voided Child

Emotions are the foundations of living. Our feelings allow us to experience the fullness of life, whether our circumstances are pleasant or uncomfortable. Being attuned to our emotions means engaging in rich and rewarding relationships and experiences that make us more interesting people.

However, many people cannot be in touch with their emotional selves. These unfortunate souls see life through tainted, grey lenses, oblivious to the brilliance and depth that emotions could bring to their lives. This lack of an emotional spectrum robs them of seeing and experiencing what life really could offer by way of relationships and joy. And that is the case with Robert (Figure 7.1).

At 28, Robert had never been married. He worked as a taxi driver and came to counseling to resolve a sex addiction that involved heavy porn use and visiting prostitutes. Robert suffered from social anxiety and demonstrated low self-worth.

The youngest of three children, he was bullied by his siblings and felt ignored by his parents.

"As far back as I can remember, my brother and sister made my life a living hell," Robert said during his first counseling session. *"I was beaten on a number of occasions and can recall hiding in the bathroom as they banged on the door threatening to kill me."*

Sharing Emotions Is Not Safe

Robert often went to his parents for help but was shunned on each occasion. His parents offered no comfort or solution for his emotional distress. Instead, they added to it by delivering the message, *"you're just too emotionally sensitive."*

"Grow up, Robert, all siblings fight," his father told him. *"Stop acting like a baby it is so pathetic how sensitive you are."*

And there was no support coming from his mother either. *"Robert, if you are going to complain every time something bothers you, no one is going to want to be around you,"* she told him in a rather heartless manner. *"You must learn to keep your feelings to yourself and solve your problems. The truth is no one is going to care about your problems. Fix them yourself."*

You may find it difficult to believe parents would be so uncaring. They probably believed they were teaching Robert to be tough and to stand on his own, but in reality, they encouraged the young boy to shut off his feelings to protect himself from additional disappointment.

"When I realised it was pointless going to them, I just suffered in silence," he remarked, shaking his head slowly. *"At first, I learned to keep my feelings to myself, and over time there were fewer feelings that I experienced."*

As an overweight child, Robert was also ridiculed throughout his school years. *"Not a day went by without someone calling me 'fat boy' or other nasty comments,"* he recalled. *"For*

DOI: 10.4324/9781003406013-7

Figure 7.1

a while, I would lock myself in the boys' bathroom at lunchtime and sob. But after I decided to stop feeling, their words no longer mattered. I brushed them aside and kept walking."

The Pursuit of Comfort

Food was Robert's source of comfort and served as a distraction from the underlying emotional pain. It was in ninth grade; he found another escape – pornography.

"I will never forget watching my first porn video – it made me forget about my futile existence and transported me into a world of bliss," he remembered with a slight smile. *"It all felt safe – food, porn, and not recognizing my emotions."*

But Robert's emotions did not go away, instead, they were repressed and stirring in his Inner Child. When bullied, rather than experiencing shame and humiliation, Robert suffered a low level of anxiety, which he medicated through food and porn. Since he had dealt with anxiety since childhood, Robert was often unaware of its presence and compulsively moved to his addictive behaviors for relief.

As the years went by, Robert's need for additional stimulation to quiet his anxiety increased, and he started to visit escorts.

"I had no friends and never had a sexual encounter with a girl, and the porn was losing its stimulating effect on me," he said. *"So, I went to see an escort and lost my virginity. Although I was nervous, I felt safe. And she made me feel wanted and validated. Afterward, I cried because no one made me feel special like she did."*

As Robert mentioned, he had no friends. This is often the case for individuals who are emotionally voided. They may have casual acquaintances but rarely have good friends in their lives. And if a friend does exist, most likely, any conversations never go too deep as those who are emotionally void keep things at a 10,000-foot level.

Going from Bad to Worst

As Robert's addictions progressed, so did the consequences. The feeling of being wanted and desired was so intoxicating for a man who had turned off his emotions for all those years that he started seeing two escorts several times a week. Over 18 months, he had spent nearly all his life savings.

"I had amassed a small fortune in savings but blew it on the girls," he said. *"I went from one-hour appointments to overnight bookings that cost me thousands. I was suffering from chronic loneliness and only knew how to relieve the pain by spending time with an escort."*

Despite blasting through his savings, Robert increased his destructive behavior to maintain his addiction.

"I started pawning items and even started stealing from my family," he said. *"The last time I saw an escort, it was a setup. I was beaten up and robbed at knifepoint. As I walked back home, I knew this had to stop. I was either going to be killed or end up in jail."*

Finding a New Hope

Robert entered treatment and began his addiction recovery shortly after being attacked. In therapy, he learned to sit and process his emotional discomfort, understanding his feelings would not kill him. He started focusing on unresolved childhood pain points, including bullying, isolation, and unsupportive and neglectful parents.

"It was very intimidating at first to focus on my childhood pain," Robert said after more than a year into his treatment process. *"But over time, it became easier, and I have worked hard to break away from the coping strategy I developed to repress my emotions. I am learning to feel, and it's very different."*

Robert also gained insight into how his troubled childhood drove him to behaviors that ultimately became addictive. With this new knowledge, he learned how to stop avoiding emotional discomfort and shift those toxic feelings toward rational thinking, preventing him from seeking escapes using food and porn. Instead, Robert was confronting his emotions and making healthier decisions.

"It all makes sense," he continued. *"Because I stopped feeling, I was zoning out first with food, then porn, and finally escorts. It was never about the sex; it was my need for emotional connection. But that was costly attention. Now I connect in healthier ways and pursue a life of sexual integrity."*

After tipping the scale at 340 pounds, Robert lost 75 pounds in a year and aimed to lose 100 more. He joined a men's support group and was recently asked to be a facilitator. He also joined Emotions Anonymous and is learning more techniques to identify and express his feelings.

Key Characteristics of the Emotionally Voided Child

What key characteristics explain the development of the Emotionally Voided Child? These children:

- Do not receive the guidance needed in the early stages of childhood development to connect emotionally with others successfully.

- Receive messages that feelings are not important or unsafe to express.
- Do not experience a role model at home that demonstrates authentic emotional intimacy.
- Do not know how to validate others, so they are very defensive.
- Learn to connect by doing things for others.
- They are present but not engaged.
- Fearful of saying the wrong thing; not knowing what to say.
- Their comments will be ignored or dismissed.

A Low Emotional IQ

Individuals with low emotional IQ will find it difficult to process and express emotions. They will also struggle to recognise and adequately manage the feelings of others – they become exasperated and anxious when put in environments that require them to provide or receive emotional engagement. As a result, they avoid engaging in emotional intimacy, using excuses such as *"I don't know what to say"* or *"I am afraid I will say the wrong thing."*

However, in many cases, these folks are not avoiding, they are simply oblivious to what is involved with emotional intimacy. Many would not recognise emotional intimacy if it ran them over. Here are some behaviors you can expect from an individual with a low emotional IQ.

1 They cannot identify what they are "truly" feeling. These individuals can tell you when they're angry, sad, afraid, or happy. But those are emotions everyone can experience and are used to protect us from dealing with vulnerable emotions. Individuals with a solid emotional IQ can drill down from the initial emotions and identify their deeper feelings. But those with a low emotional IQ cannot process and describe their more robust feelings. For example, an angry person may be feeling dismissed or cheated. But instead of recognising their genuine emotion and expressing the hurt associated with it, they react in anger. In many cases, this develops when parents do not help their children give words to their emotions.
2 Even if these individuals can identify their true emotions, they will have difficulty expressing them. People with low emotional IQs were never taught how to appropriately process and communicate their feelings. Instead, they were encouraged or demanded to keep their emotions to themselves. Somewhere along the line, like Robert, they've received the message "sharing your feelings results in trouble."
3 What is most annoying for a partner of someone with a low emotional IQ is their inability to recognise and effectively deal with the emotions of others. These folks cannot read people's emotional signs, especially non-verbal cues. They also cannot be empathic listeners and instead try to "fix" problems. They often conflict with their partners because they must shut down emotional dialogues to avoid anxiety. We usually refer to these individuals as being emotionally tone-deaf.
4 These folks also tend to shift emotional conversations toward themselves. For example, if a man's wife says, *"It was a crazy day, and my head is spinning,"* instead of asking her what happened to leave her in a mentally exhausted state, he will say something along the lines of *"I know what you're feeling. I also had an insane day."* He doesn't pick up the fact she is trying to be vulnerable and looking to engage in conversation to get a sympathetic ear. His inability to do this will, in turn, send her the indirect message, *"I don't care about your day,"* which is not what he meant to do.

5 Individuals with low emotional IQ may find making and maintaining friendships exceedingly difficult. Part of the reason for this is their quest for solitude. A woman who must engage with people throughout the workday will become very drained and have little energy for her family, never mind friends. She will give the impression of being aloof, although that is not her intent. A part of her would like to have friends, but the thought of putting in the effort to cultivate them is exhausting. In cases where she may have friends, these relationships are kept at a 10,000-foot level and rarely, if ever, result in emotionally meaningful conversations.

Confusing Physical Intimacy for Emotional

Having been guys (Eddie and Nathan) with low emotional IQs, we know first-hand the struggle to connect with others emotionally. We thought we did. But for us, sexual and non-sexual touch was our number one way to demonstrate emotional intimacy. Our erroneous belief was, *"you show someone you love them by the way you make them feel physically."* This is another significant complaint partners often broach.

"The only time he touches or acknowledges me is when he wants to have sex," said Barbara, whose husband is addicted to pornography and visits strip clubs regularly. *"I start to cringe whenever he comes near me because I know what he's looking for. It leaves me feeling used, and he doesn't understand that."*

Emotionally Voided Children

Inner children HATE feeling any emotions except those that are pleasurable. Remember, their goal is always to seek comfort. For individuals with a low emotional IQ, their inner children are hypervigilant and on the alert for troubling emotions experienced both internally and those expressed by others. They are on guard to sound the alarm that danger is lurking – *"emotions are in the house, and it's time to jump ship!"*

To the Inner Child, emotions are destructive and must be avoided at all costs. These kids were raised in homes where they saw little emotional intimacy expressed. There was only moderate or often no physical touch displayed between parents or siblings. A hug or kiss was rare to find. And if it did come, it was usually quick or half-hearted. The child raised in this environment doesn't have the model needed to learn how to be emotionally engaging. Therefore, this Inner Child will be severely disadvantaged when dealing with emotions and learning to connect intimately with others.

In her cutting-edge book, *Running on Empty: Overcome Your Childhood Emotional Neglect*, Dr. Jonice Webb provides several explanations for developing a low emotional IQ.

- This is the child whose parents didn't teach emotional-processing skills because they struggled to identify their emotions. Feelings were never discussed in this home, and if any were presented, they were quickly shut down or dismissed. *"When your prom date stands you up, your family shows their support by making an effort never to speak of it,"* says Dr. Webb in providing an example of what this child went through at home. *"Or they tease you about it relentlessly, never seeming to notice or care how very mortified you are. The result is these individuals don't learn how to be self-aware,"* she continues. *"They don't learn that their feelings are real or important. And they are not taught how to feel, sit with, talk about, or express emotions."*
- Other kids struggle with their emotional IQ because their parents were not good at managing and controlling their own emotions, therefore, they were unable to teach

children how to manage and control theirs. *"When you get in trouble at school for calling your teacher 'a jerk,' your parents do not ask you what was going on or why you lost your temper that way,"* Dr. Webb explains. *"They don't teach you how you could have handled that situation differently. Instead, they ground you, yell at you, or blame it on your teacher, letting you off the hook. These kids don't learn how to control or manage their feelings or difficult situations."*

• For these children, it is about receiving the wrong message about themselves and the world due to insensitive behavior from parents and family members who simply are emotionally clueless. *"Take, for example, that your parents act as if you're lazy because they haven't noticed that it's your anxiety that holds you back from doing things,"* says Dr. Webb. *"The result is these individuals go into adulthood with the wrong voices in their heads. 'You're lazy,' 'You're weak,' say the Voices of Low Emotional Intelligence at every opportunity."*

What You Feel vs. What Is Real

Individuals with low emotional intelligence lack awareness of their surroundings and other people. They spend their lives running with their heads down, oblivious to the rest of the world, while stuck in their own thoughts. To become emotionally intimate, they will need to learn to focus and be aware of the needs and desires of those around them while recognising opportunities to engage in a genuine community.

They also need to evaluate the Inner Child's emotions and ask, *"This is what he feels, but what is real?"* Because as you go through the Inner Child Process, you will discover what your Inner Child "feels" vs. what is "real" are often two very different things. And the reason for that is your Inner Child's emotions are based solely on fear.

Fear of Rejection

Those who grow up not learning to engage with others in a healthy way emotionally will often become anxious when placed in social environments. They lack the confidence to be able to carry on conversations. More importantly, they subconsciously worry about rejection if they allow people to become emotionally close. So, what's the Inner Child's solution? They'll do the following:

• Keep people at a distance.
• Learn to be present but not engaged.
• Maintain a low profile and stay out of sight.
• Don't share thoughts and opinions unless it is absolutely necessary.
• Always keep your answers short and to the point; too many spoken words can get you in trouble.

When you talk to these individuals about emotional intimacy, most look like a deer caught in headlights. They have no idea what is about to hit them. They only know it sounds dangerous. Ironically, these people crave emotional intimacy and connection – they just don't realise it.

However, they are extremely limited in what they can give and receive in the way of emotional intimacy, and this can be immensely frustrating to loved ones looking for connection and engagement.

If you are not taught how to engage others in a healthy emotional manner, you are likely to feel uncomfortable and awkward when placed in circumstances that require you to interact.

In their best-selling book *How We Love*, Milan and Kay Yerkovich point out that we don't learn to love when we start dating or get married. We learn to love in our family of origin.

"What bothers you most about your spouse is undoubtedly related to painful experiences from childhood and lack of training in addressing the true challenges of marriage. Your marriage problems did not begin in your marriage! You and your spouse are doing the dance steps you learned in childhood. For each of you, a pattern of relating was set in motion long before you met."

So, what happens when a young girl or boy doesn't witness healthy love in their family of origin because parents are too distracted or negligent in engaging with them? They will most likely end up shutting off their emotional pipeline and failing to develop the social skills needed to be affectionate and attentive partners.

They will also be quick to retreat when emotions start to emerge during conversations. A major complaint from partners is the emotionally void person is too quick to withdraw from the family.

"It's like clockwork," says Mara, whose husband Chuck has used online pornography since its inception in the mid-90s. *"One minute he's with us, and the next minute he's burying himself in his phone or other electronics. It's frustrating because it communicates to the kids and me that we are not important or annoying. It's like something clicks in his brain, and he runs away from us."*

Inner Child Theory in Action

A vital requirement for those in addiction recovery is to establish techniques to reduce the anxiety experienced when emotions appear, so these individuals can remain engaged with others instead of simply being present.

Letter writing is a helpful tool used within the Inner Child Recovery Process. By acknowledging the pain and suffering your Inner Child experienced at the hands of others, you facilitate the process of healing and integration within your true self.

Letters are written to parents, siblings, peers, and anyone else with whom your Inner Child is still troubled today.

"In therapy, I learned to sort through the emotions associated with my anxiety by writing letters to many of the people who hurt my Inner Child and me," said Claire, a 41-year-old divorcee recovering from alcoholism. *"I discovered the emotions presented by my inner little girl were always fearful. So, I directed those fearful emotions to rational thinking and repeatedly saw that the circumstances I was dealing with were nothing to fear. My little girl was focusing on painful memories that she thought matched what was going on in my life today. But she was wrong, and now I can tell her I know that and move forward despite the anxiety I may feel."*

Writing a letter to your Inner Child explaining their fears are unfounded, and the negative narratives they believe are untrue can also be a significant stepping stone to helping ease the child's concerns.

Hank's Letter

Hank grew up being compared to his siblings, who were top in their school classes. A student who mainly achieved "Cs," he was frequently reminded by his parents and teachers of his less-than-stellar academic pursuits.

"I grew up thinking I was not very smart," said Hank, a primary care physician who dealt with a gambling addiction. *"My parents constantly criticised me, and I never felt good about*

myself. I didn't date anyone in high school, and I had few friends because I did not know how to socialise with others.

"But everything changed when I got to college," he continued. *"I had great academic success and went to medical school to be a physician. I also married a beautiful woman. But being emotionally voided, I never learned to regulate my mood and was prone to verbal outbursts."*

Hank's anger problem got him removed from the staff of several hospitals. Those setbacks stirred up the negative belief that he was stupid. So, he turned to gambling to turn off that noise.

"I always loved sports," he recalled. *"So, I started gambling on baseball, football, and basketball. I had some success but far too many failures. My mind was not focused on my work because I was researching the best bets for that day. It reached a point where I lost more than $50K in one year. That is when I knew things needed to change."*

During therapy, a key event that turned things around for Hank was writing a letter to his younger self (this inner child). Hank expressed empathy for the child he knew had grown up, thinking he was destined for a life of failure. Hank pointed out to his Inner Child that life was difficult as a kid due to the neglect from his parents, who:

- Did not provide him with the skills (attunement, trust, empathy, emotion identification, and mood regulation) needed to be emotionally developed.
- Did not provide the encouragement and praise necessary to build his confidence.
- Eroded his self-worth with their criticism of him and comparison to his siblings.

In writing the letter to his Inner Child, Hank saw for the first time that he was a child filled with the potential to accomplish good things, but he was not given a chance due to his parents' neglectful ways. He achieved his potential only when he left his parents and the toxic environment they had created. Unfortunately, his emotional under-development and inability to manage his anger sent him back to a crisis-filled life.

Vulnerability: Taking a Risk

Managing your Inner Child's fearful emotions is critical for your addiction recovery. Fear is what got you in this mess, to begin with, and it is fear as a child that drove you to lose touch with your emotions. The fear embedded within your Inner Child can be managed, but the first step is recognising it exists. Once you've done this, you can confront the fear by committing to be vulnerable and sharing with someone safe.

You must learn to take risks. Healthy risks.

Let's be honest; it's not like you are unfamiliar with risk-taking. You probably took many risks when it involved your addiction. And it is a good bet that many of those risks have cost you dearly. The danger we are discussing is significantly different from the risk of vulnerability. More importantly, the result can lead to tremendous positive dividends. You may finally understand what it feels like to be alive. Doesn't that sound appealing?

Kid Talk

So, what does your emotionally voided Inner Child need to hear from you? We're going to give you some practical tools to teach and comfort your child. This kid doesn't believe emotions are safe, so you must provide him with insights into the benefits of emotions. Let him know that sharing feelings can ease burdens and decrease the chances of experiencing stress-related physiological problems like muscle pain, tension headaches, high blood pressure, and anxiety, to mention but a few. Remember, the Inner Child's goal is comfort, so let him know that comfort can be found in sharing emotions.

He doesn't believe people are safe. He is frightened that sharing emotions will result in rejection. This comes back to the concept of taking risks. Tell him you will "go slow" when sharing emotions to see how individuals react. Over time, you will expand sharing with those who prove trustworthy. Discuss with him how being emotionally vulnerable can help strengthen relationships and allow you to experience more love and life.

It is your responsibility to make the child feel at ease, and you will accomplish this by telling him you understand what needs to be done to address the situation and that you will handle it. This will stop him from feeling like he did when you were younger, that he was on his own and there was no one there for him. Let him know that has changed. You get the idea.

Your Inner Child may have received the message that being emotional is a sign of weakness. While you can't provide him with absolute certainty your emotions will always be validated, the emphasis needs to focus on being empowered despite the outcome. Sharing means we have taken control. He will like that message.

Core Emotional Triggers of the Emotionally Voided Child

This is only a partial list, and you may identify additional triggers. Remember, these emotions occur based on the way your Inner Child perceives a current situation. However, the kid's perception of events may be inaccurate.

I'm a Disappointment	I'm Afraid
I'm Numb	I Feel Lost
I'm Different in a Bad Way	I'm Not Important
I'm Overwhelmed	I'm Lonely

Workbook

1 Do you **resonate** with the Emotionally Void Child?

   Yes ☐   No ☐

2 If yes, why do you **resonate** with this child? What were the messages you received about sharing emotions when growing up? Was this encouraged or frowned upon? Write your story. Be as specific as possible.

   _____
   _____
   _____
   _____
   _____

3 Which of the following do you **struggle** with?

   A I don't know what I "truly" feel ☐
   B I have a difficult time expressing my emotions ☐
   C I have a difficult time recognising and effectively dealing with the emotions of others ☐
   D I tend to shift the emotional conversation toward myself ☐
   E I find it very difficult to know what to say during conversations ☐
   F I find it very difficult to make and maintain friendships ☐
   G All the above ☐

4 Do you believe you **learned to cut off** some, or all, of your emotions apart from sadness, anger, happiness, and fear?

   Yes ☐   No ☐   Not sure ☐

5 If you answered **yes** to question 4, why did you do that? What circumstances or individual(s) led you to take that action?

   _____
   _____
   _____
   _____
   _____

6 How would you **rate** your Emotional IQ?

1 = very immature   10 = very mature

0	1	2	3	4	5	6	7	8	9	10

7 What prevents you from being **vulnerable** with your emotions?

A I have no idea how to be vulnerable ☐
B I do not want to be vulnerable ☐
C I don't know what I feel ☐
D I am afraid I will be dismissed ☐
E I am afraid I will be ridiculed ☐
F Other _____

8 How do you believe the **inability** to emotionally connect impacts your relationships?

_____
_____
_____
_____
_____

9 When **faced with conflict**, what do you do most often?

A Become aggressive ☐
B Withdraw ☐
C Say little or nothing (be passive) ☐

10 Which of these Core Emotional Triggers **resonate** with you?

I am a disappointment ☐   I am always wrong ☐   I feel lost ☐
No one needs me ☐   I feel disappointed ☐   I don't fit in ☐
I am not important ☐   I am different in a bad way ☐
I need to feel numb ☐   Other: _____

11 Taking each trigger, **explain** why you selected it and how it **originated**. Again, write your story and be as specific as possible.

_____
_____
_____
_____
_____

12   How can you healthily respond to these triggers? What **ideas** do you have for doing this?

_____

_____

_____

_____

_____

13   Well done! Now **comment** below: what are two key points you learned in this chapter? Be as specific as possible in your answers.

_____

_____

_____

_____

_____

Chapter 8

The Need for Control Child

We all know how comfortable it is being around control freaks. Their desire to manage all details and inform us of the right and wrong approach to things can leave us constricted and lacking a voice (see Figure 8.1).

If you are a control freak, you may not realise you can make others anxious. But you do. It is a characteristic that is ingrained in you and is tapped into like second nature. But what is behind the makeup of individuals who strive to maintain control at the cost of alienating others? Well, let's look at Dee's story.

Grooming the Need for Control Child

Dee came to counseling with a pornography addiction. At age 26, she had no children and lived with her partner Alice. They had been together for five years. Addiction ran in Dee's family, with her mother an alcoholic and her father a sex addict.

"Childhood was grim, mom was constantly pissed, and dad was messing around with other women," said Dee, who looked at least a decade older than her age. *"I remember when I was seven, coming home from school and seeing my mother passed out on the kitchen floor. I thought she was dead. I was so scared. I later found out she was drunk."*

Dee's father was at work most of the time; however, when he got home, the tension ran high between him and his wife.

"They fought all the time," Dee said. *"And I mean knock-down, nasty fights. My sister and I would hide to avoid being hit by the items thrown about. But there was no escaping the noise."*

And there was no escaping the wrath of mom. With dad out chasing female conquests, Dee and her sister took the verbal and physical hits that mom would have liked to give her husband. The intensity of her anger increased when she was drunk, which was often.

"My sister and I made every attempt to keep my mother happy and calm", Dee said. *"My sister and I made sure anything that would anger her was taken care of. On top of that, I tried to stay one step ahead of her guessing what she needed.*

"Keeping mom content was very challenging and often did not work, despite our best efforts. So, we continued to take her abuse, Dee continued. *At some point, when I was around 13, I discovered porn and soon found it was a good way to forget about my awful life"*.

After graduating high school, Dee left home and moved in with some friends. She took a job as a waitress and started to get her life together. *"I had to escape that madhouse, and I did the first chance I had,"* she said. *"It was such a relief to be away from mom, but that did not stop me from watching porn. I watch multiple times throughout the day and masturbate, including at work. It helps me whenever the restaurant is super busy and I feel out of control. It allows me to cope but only for a short time."*

DOI: 10.4324/9781003406013-8

Figure 8.1

Dee did not date in High School because she was attracted to women and didn't want to stand out among her peers. Several years after graduating, she met Alice, who is 13 years older. At first, Alice enjoyed watching porn with Dee, but after a few years, she started to get annoyed that Dee wanted to watch it whenever they had sex. It became a conflict between them, but it did not stop Dee from watching.

"I stopped watching porn at home and told Alice I was done with it," Dee explained. *"But I have not stopped. I still do it at work and in my car. That is until she found out, which is why I am here. She says I have a decision to make, porn or her. And I want her."*

Inner Child Theory in Action

During therapy, Dee discovered her addiction served as a coping mechanism to handle stressful circumstances she had no control. *"I can recall working a shift, and my replacement would call out, and I was told I have to do a double,"* she said. *"Within 10 minutes, I would be in the women's room looking at porn images and masturbating. And I would need to do that at least once an hour to get through the shift."*

Through the unresolved childhood pain points of a terrorising abusive mother and a father who offered no protection, Dee grieved her lost childhood. And she learned new coping mechanism required when her Inner Child started to feel things were threatening. She learned to process her uncomfortable emotions and evaluate them through rational thinking. She discovered that often what she felt versus what was reality were two very different things. Therefore, she needed to stop reacting based solely on her emotional state and start leaning on her wise mind.

"It's fascinating to understand how much our inner child drives our actions," Dee said. *"My little girl is so fearful that we will not be able to handle the circumstances we face, and that makes sense since we grew up surrounded by fear."*

"I am glad that I was able to see why I was engrossed in porn and able to break free of it," she continued. *"And so is Alice. And that is what makes me most happy."*

Harry's Story

Harry was dealt a bad hand. To say his childhood was chaotic would be an understatement. He was the first of four children, and one of his siblings was a brother with autism. His father suffered from chronic depression, which prevented him from being steadily employed. Instead, if you needed to find Harry's dad, you had to look no further than the bedroom, where he spent endless hours watching television.

Meanwhile, his mother was forced to work two jobs to support the family. And when she was not working, you could typically find her sitting on a barstool at the tavern across the street from their apartment. It was not a hallmark family.

As the oldest child, it naturally fell upon Harry to become his siblings' caregiver at the expense of his childhood. Due to home life demands, Harry had to forgo the youthful activities most kids enjoy. He traded in friends and school experiences for the role of a surrogate parent. Harry would miss out on being a child and teenager. He suffered a completely lost childhood.

"I was an adult way before my time," he said with a low voice and a terrible sense of sadness. *"But there was no one there to care for the others. Dad was always locked in his bedroom, and mom was never home. No one ever told me I had to care for my siblings; I just took it upon myself. However, if I didn't step up, we probably would have been sent to foster care, and I couldn't allow that to happen.*

"But in reality, I was dying every day," he continued as he slowly monitored his words. *"I am unsure how I got schoolwork done with everything else I needed to do. But I did. Looking back, it seems impossible for a kid to raise three other kids. But that was my life. There was nothing else."*

Handling the responsibilities of an adult while trying to be a productive student caused Harry chronic anxiety, a condition he still deals with today. Facing an environment that would be challenging for two parents was overwhelming for the young boy, who often felt over his head trying to manage a household, schoolwork, and child-rearing responsibilities.

"I was always worried I would mess up and something would happen to one of my brothers or my sister," he recalled. *"Especially Arthur, who had autism. He was a handful, and I had no idea what was wrong with him. I didn't know what autism was. It was scary.*

"I felt as though I was constantly living in a state of fear," he continued. *"Whether I was going to pass my classes or ensure everyone was fed. There was ALWAYS something that needed to be done and ALWAYS something that I worried I wasn't doing. I have been on anti-anxiety meds most of my adult life."*

Seeking Escapes

The chaos in the noisy, disorganised, and cluttered apartment often left Harry feeling he failed in his self-appointed responsibilities. Harry thought he was disappointing his mother, father, siblings, and himself. It was a gigantic emotional burden placed on a young boy's shoulders, and he often thought about running away to escape his feelings of failure.

You may equate "chaotic" with "abusive," but that is not always the case. Yes, abusive environments are chaotic, but not all chaotic environments are abusive. Instead, they are viewed as neglected.

Harry eventually found two escapes from the emotional pandemonium that swirled through his head and the endless responsibilities he faced – control and pornography. He learned that to manage the hellish environment, control was essential. Out of self-preservation, Harry became a metaphorical drill sergeant. He established a rigid and uncompromising climate in the home and among his siblings to create stability. Each was given tasks that needed to be completed daily, and there was no room for non-compliance.

"I was at a loss because no one was showing me how to raise kids," Harry said as he leaned back on the couch, seeming exhausted just talking about the situation. *"I had to get them to listen to me, especially Arthur, so I decided to become a hardhead with all of them. I was determined not to fail."*

With this new approach to running the home, Harry addressed non-compliance with the rules by doling out various punishments, which included physical attacks. Soon his younger siblings came to understand there was a new sheriff in town. They soon discovered that doing chores was a better option than beatings. Harry hated who he was becoming but saw no other solution.

Harry ran a tight ship at home as he entered his teen years, although this came at a high cost. His brothers and sister feared and hated him. He had no social life, and his grades at school were suffering. While he could institute a structure at home that created some sense of control, Harry's anxiety was still running amok emotionally. Enter escape number two.

At age 13, Harry came across some of his father's pornographic magazines. The images he saw were incredibly stimulating for a child whose mind focused mainly on dealing with the next crisis. He soon discovered pornography was an intoxicating distraction from the frenzy surrounding him at home.

"It sounds crazy, but pornography was like a light in all of the darkness," he explained. *"It was one of the few times I could recall that was pleasurable. I know it was wrong, but I needed it back then. It kept me sane."*

Harry soon discovered he could control his anxiety by taking breaks to view pornography and masturbate. The invigoration pornography provided kept at bay the distressing and uneasy feelings and thoughts that continuously plagued him. It became a source of relief for a young boy in circumstances he should have never faced. His parents' failure to carry out their responsibilities led him to seek what was to become an addiction that would subsequently cause severe issues in his romantic relationships.

Individuals like Harry use sexual activity to maintain stability in their lives, which provides security. They use control to remain safe. Safe from what you may ask? Good question. They are seeking sanctuary from the chronic emotional distress that presents in the form of anxiety or depression. In most cases, these individuals have no clue regarding the true nature of their emotional turmoil.

Unrealised Stress

Listen to Harry today as an adult, and he will tell you his anxiety is more a sense of restlessness. That is why he continually stays busy, running from one activity to the next. But he still has no idea what he is running from. The two core emotional triggers his Inner Child seeks to escape are *"I'm a disappointment"* and *"I don't measure up."* But again, Harry is unaware of the emotional triggers that activate his Inner Child. Instead, he thinks his crazy schedule is just an attempt to keep his life organised and controlled. However, his life is anything but harmonious.

After high school, Harry left home and found a low-level construction job. His strong work ethic helped him succeed in the workplace, and he later started his own business. His need for control has led to financial success, which is good.

But his personal life is anything but prosperous. Harry has been divorced twice and is working hard to keep together a third marriage, hanging on by a string. Why has he experienced so much destruction in his relationships? Because he is a raging sex addict who has betrayed every woman he has ever dated or married.

Harry acts out daily with sexual activities ranging from high-class escorts to sexual encounters in sleazy adult bookstores. If he is not focused on his business, Harry's seeking sex to drown the faint, chaotic background noise (that he cannot physically hear) forever playing in his head that he's not good enough and failure is right around the corner.

"I have always wondered why I cheat," he said. *"I assumed it was a character flaw. I never knew until we started therapy that I was using sex to bury my insecurity of failing. I wish I had known all this earlier. It would have saved me and others a lot of grief."*

Harry's Inner Child

How is this for irony? A sexually addicted man who is fixated on control is uncontrollable when dealing with sex. And we could say the same for any addiction – alcohol, drugs, gambling, food, or work – you name it.

As we have been pointing out, the rationale behind this craziness is he doesn't understand the true nature of his anxiousness. At his core, Harry's Inner Child is fearful and overwhelmed. He worries chaos will develop at any moment, and life will spin out of control.

The kid fears failure and directs Harry to take control of situations and, if necessary, use unhealthy sexual activities to distract from potential negative feelings.

There are two reasons why our inner children may be activated when experiencing circumstances that leave them feeling powerless.

1 They see control as a protective device to generate feelings that life is orderly and to prevent bad things from happening.
2 They are seeking to avoid the painful emotions associated with being micromanaged and controlled.

Some kids grow up in homes governed by rules, rules, and more rules. A rigid environment can feel like a vice tightening around your throat, leaving you gasping for air. You have no say in your life and are given a limited or no voice. Life is not your own – instead, it is managed by others.

"My father was a tyrant," said Sasha, who became addicted to opiates after a motorcycle crash fractured her spine. *"There was one way for everything – his way. I, my mother, and my two brothers had to adhere to everything he wanted. We had no say in our lives."*

Children living under these conditions are not allowed to make decisions or share their opinions. Instead, they meet the needs and wants of others to conform to the family system. While in some cases, the parents' intentions are to provide healthy guidelines required for their kids to develop into productive adults. But instead, they are creating individuals filled with resentment and anger. In other circumstances, parents are evil people seeking to manipulate and use their children.

Key Characteristics of the Need for Control Child

What key characteristics explain the development of the Need For Control Child?

- Raised in hectic and chaotic environments or a rigid and rules-oriented environment.
- Negative consequences always landed on them.
- Work to not add to the chaos surrounding them.
- Their quest is to seek order to reduce anxiety.
- Seek distractions for circumstances in which they have no control.

For this Inner Child, control is the glue that holds everything in place and keeps chaos at bay. Maintaining control of their environment provides these children with peace and calm. The Inner Child will do anything to obtain this level of comfort, including leading us toward behaviors that can turn into addictions.

The "Why" Behind Control

We do not need to be in control to have comfort, which is the primary objective of our Inner Child. They recall trying to survive in an abusive, chaotic, or rigid atmosphere experienced at home or elsewhere, such as at school or in the neighborhood. And when similar circumstances arise today, they refuse to allow us to go back and sit with those painful emotions. In their limited, emotionally focused world, maintaining control is the answer to creating stability. *"If we're in charge, bad things can't happen to us"* is their worldview.

Due to our lack of awareness, we yield to our Inner Child's worldview, and the result is escaping via behaviors to avoid facing troubling emotions. Again, they are running the show. And we are not better because of it.

WHAT YOU "FEEL" VERSUS WHAT IS "REAL" ARE USUALLY DIFFERENT THINGS

When you allow your Inner Child to lead, you are not viewing your emotions and thoughts through the lens of truth. Instead, you elect to listen to the distorted views of a hurt child who will seek comfort at any cost. You are listening to and following an adolescent voice when you need to hear and follow a voice of wisdom. Your adult voice.

Remember, inner children do not trust people. They are somewhat paranoid and on the alert for those trying to hurt them. They equate control with security to prevent that from happening and ultimately make incorrect assumptions. But then again, they don't know any better – they're just kids.

Best-selling author John Bradshaw, who wrote one of the premier books about the Inner Child, *Homecoming: Reclaiming and Healing Your Inner Child,* noted the confused mind of our young companion.

"A person who never learned to trust confuses intensity with intimacy, obsession with care, and control with security," says Bradshaw in his defining the Inner Child.

When our Inner Child feels the comfortable state of harmony is being disrupted (via a core emotional trigger), they seek to protect themselves. If we allow the Inner Child to go unchecked, it will lead us to make emotionally charged decisions that have little to do with cognitive or rational thinking. When a child determines the course of action an adult should take to reduce anxiety, you can bet it will most likely lead to destructive consequences.

The first step to recovery is realising you are not in control. The addiction has disempowered you. The key is to face our unresolved childhood pain points and develop the skills required to process those wounds and empower yourself. It is time for you to start running the show.

Kid Talk

Here are some practical tools to teach and comfort the Inner Child who lacks control. Remember, we are trying to soothe and not criticise or belittle him/her. You want to determine your Inner Child's negative narratives. If you recall, negative narratives are the lies we tell ourselves about ourselves. You start by speaking with the Inner Child to uncover the negative narratives they believe.

Once you have determined those narratives, ponder how they may have developed. Where did your child first hear them? Who or what was responsible for their development?

Once you have that vital information, you can start placing each negative narrative in front of the mirror of truth and ask yourself, *"although I feel this way, what is reality?"* and *"is this an accurate description of myself?"*

Core Emotional Triggers of the Need for Control Child

This is only a partial list and you may identify additional triggers. Remember, these emotions occur based on the way your Inner Child perceives a current situation. However, the kid's perception of events may be inaccurate.

I am Powerless	I Feel Weak
I Have Been Cheated	I am Not Safe
I Have Been Victimised	I am Helpless
I am a Disappointment	I Do Not Measure Up

Workbook

1 Do you **resonate** with the Need for Control Child?

   Yes ☐   No ☐

2 If yes, why do you **resonate** with this child? What conditions left you feeling you needed to be in control growing up? Did this occur at home, in school, with peers, or with others? Write your story. Be as specific as possible.

   _____
   _____
   _____
   _____
   _____

3 Do you think the need for **control** is a factor that has driven you to engage in addictive behaviors?

   Yes ☐   No ☐

4 If you answered yes to question 3, why do you **believe** this is a factor?

   _____
   _____
   _____
   _____
   _____

5 What **value** does the attempt to maintain control bring to your life?

   _____
   _____
   _____
   _____
   _____

6 Is it difficult for you to **trust others?** If yes, explain why.

   _____
   _____
   _____
   _____

The first step to recovery is realising you are not in control. However, you have the most crucial role to play in your recovery. The extent to which you take responsibility and put in the work needed will determine your success or failure.

7 Which of these Core Emotional Triggers **resonate** with you?

I feel powerless ☐   I feel weak ☐   I have been cheated ☐
I have been victimised ☐   I am not safe ☐   I am helpless ☐
I do not measure up ☐   I am overwhelmed ☐   I feel trapped ☐
Other: _____

8 Taking each trigger, **explain** why you selected it and how it originated. Again, write your story and be as specific as possible.

_____
_____
_____
_____
_____

9 How can you effectively **soothe** the anxiety of your Inner Child when things are out of control? Be creative in your thinking.

_____
_____
_____
_____
_____

10 Well done! Now **comment** below: what are two key points you learned in this chapter? Be as specific as possible in your answers.

_____
_____
_____
_____
_____

Chapter 9

The Entitled-Spiteful Child

Many of you will be tempted to skip this chapter, feeling it will not pertain to you. However, we recommend you take the time to review the circumstances surrounding the Entitled-Spiteful Child (see Figure 9.1) before deciding whether the kid belongs, or not, among your inner children.

It is not uncommon for many who go through the Inner Child Model to write off this child, only to come back and realise this kid has played an important role in their lives. And even if that is not the case with you, at least our writing did not go to waste.

Life is not fair. That is the battle cry of the Entitled-Spiteful Child, who believes everyone and everything is against him/her. These Inner Children cannot understand why people make their lives so difficult when they want to get along with everyone. This Entitled-Spiteful Inner Child is very different from children who have an entitlement mentality and believe rules do not apply to them. These children also have a "you owe me" attitude and strong narcissistic tendencies. But this is not the makeup of *our* Entitled-Spiteful Inner Child.

Our Inner Child was made to feel unappreciated or devalued. Their sense of entitlement came from being exposed to circumstances they found to be unfair. They have experienced a great deal of confusion and frustration trying to understand the insensitivity and, at times, the cruelty of others.

Bernice's Story

The middle of three children growing up, Bernice felt caught in a whirlpool of turmoil in her home. Her older sister was a bully who used physically abusive threats to keep Bernice under her control. Her younger brother falsely pointed the finger of blame at Bernice whenever he did something wrong. Being the favorite, his accusations usually were accepted unconditionally by his parents, and Bernice endured many undeserving punishments.

"There were few safe moments living in my house," Bernice said during her first session. *"I was being picked on by my sister or punished by my parents for things I did not do. I thought about suicide often."*

Bernice, 35, entered counseling after completing treatment in a 90-day residential in-patient program. She struggled with alcohol and amphetamines, and this was her second stay in a long-term treatment facility.

"You're not selfish for wanting to be treated well." – Unknown

DOI: 10.4324/9781003406013-9

Figure 9.1

"I started drinking and getting high around 16," she recalled. *"I needed something to help me forget what was waiting for me at home. When I went off to college, my using intensified. It was a miracle that I could keep my grades up."*

After graduating college, Bernice got her realtor's license. Several years later, she married and had two children. During her pregnancies, Bernice quit drinking and remained dry for five years after the birth of her second child. However, the unreasonable demands of her clientele led to a resumption of using amphetamines.

"I was exhausted and needed more energy," she said. *"But the number one reason I was using was to deal with my insensitive clients. They were completely unreasonable and expected me to be available to them day and night. So, while loading myself up with uppers in the morning, I went back to drinking in the afternoon to quiet myself down."*

Wake-Up Call

Bernice's insensitive clients reminded her Inner Child of her cruel siblings and rush-to-judgment parents. Just as she abused alcohol as a teenager to escape her emotional pain, she turned to uppers and drinking to seek relief from the feeling of being taken advantage of by her clients.

"Just as I did as a teenager, I justified my using as something I deserved for the crappy way people treated me," she said. *"I was entitled to comfort myself because no one else was doing it."*

Her Inner Child was activated during any circumstance that left Bernice feeling she *"had no voice"* or was *"not being respected."*

"I was feeling that way every day," she said. *"There was no escaping it unless I got high or numbed out. This was something I was doing for myself. But the problem was my life wasn't only about me. I had a husband and children, and it took a near tragedy for me to wake up."*

"I had passed out on the couch, and my 6-year-old daughter was standing over me, holding a wrap of amphetamine," she recalls. *"As I woke up to the sound of her calling me, she asked if it was sugar. I will never forget the fear and shame I felt – my little girl holding my drugs! I immediately reached out for help."*

Inner Child Theory in Action

Following a five-day in-treatment program, Bernice visited my (Nathan) office for treatment. Our first objective was to help Bernice reduce her anxiety and understand what we "feel" is often different from what is "real." She was taught to slow down when thoughts such as *"I do not have a voice"* entered her mind. She then was taught how to sit with the uncomfortable negative noise in her mind and shift to her wise mind, where she could see the thought was irrational.

She was shown how to separate her emotions toward her family from those she felt toward her clients. This enabled her to educate and comfort her Inner Child to understand that circumstances involving her clients differed from those she experienced with her family. In dealing with clients, Bernice should have had control over the circumstances; however, she was not exercising it.

This helped Bernice slow down her erratic thinking when she felt life was unfair. In turn, she processed destructive negative thoughts that, in the past, had led her to addictive behaviors. Now she understood she was in control and could decide what actions to take when a client sought her time and energy.

Once this was accomplished, Bernice learned the importance of boundaries. She recognised that providing quality customer service did not entitle clients to have access to her 24/7.

Moving forward, when a client would be demanding, Bernice did not give into the fear of her Inner Child (*"I'm not being respected"*) and run off to use. Instead, she processed the uncomfortable emotions and used rational thinking to determine how to handle the client's request.

Bernice reports being sober for more than two years and is living a more balanced work and family life.

Key Characteristics of the Entitled-Spiteful Child

What are some key characteristics that explain the development of the Entitled-Spiteful Child? Here is a partial list of events that could lead this Inner Child to become activated:

- Falsely accused of things they didn't do
- Not believed when telling the truth
- Feeling humiliated
- Not given a voice to express their thoughts or emotions
- Being bullied
- Feeling threatened
- Feeling cheated

As children and teenagers, they had a chip on their shoulders and always looked at what could have, or should have been, instead of accepting what reality offered. It wasn't unusual for this child to feel like they always got the short end of the stick.

- The last one picked in the playground
- No one was interested in what they had to say
- Being subjected to bullying or being an outcast
- Being blamed for things they did not do
- Efforts to connect with others are not well received or met with a lack of interest

Simply put, injustice ruled these children's worlds. The experience of being slighted or rejected would lead to emotions ranging from self-pity to defiance. Their worldview became *"life's not fair."*

Soon after the initial exposure to their addiction of choice, this child learned to use it as a *reward* for the mistreatment suffered at the hands of others. Today as an adult, when a core emotional trigger appears that gives the impression things are not going your way, your Inner Child is activated and leads the way toward engaging in destructive behaviors to escape your emotional discomfort. The new worldview has become *"I deserve this."*

Kid Talk

The Entitled-Spiteful Inner Child is a tough cookie. He is the kid with an attitude, and his ability to rebel makes him extremely unsafe. So, what actions can you take to nurture this Inner Child? Here are a few ideas.

- You start with education. Your kid needs to understand that although he/she is still emotionally trapped in the times of injustice you faced, today is a new era. Even if you're still experiencing some injustice in your life, it is critical the kid understands healthy ways of dealing with it. Their *"I don't care what others think or want"* approach no longer works. It just makes things worse. So, you want to inform them that, while you understand their pain, you are taking control and will rationally sort through the situation.
- You want your child to feel your confidence in managing the distressing circumstances, which will create a sense of comfort and assurance for him/her. Let the child know you **can** run the show, and the kid can sit back and watch you work. You also may need to release some of the child's anger. The resentment the kid is experiencing has been sitting there far too long. It's time to lance the boil and let the infected wound drain.
- Spend time reviewing the most unjust events you experienced as a child that resulted in you feeling mistreated. Discuss those times with your inner kid and share your sense of pain. Help the child understand you are there and sympathise. Knowing someone cares will bring the child great comfort.

If "entitlement" is one of the reasons you identified with, it is critical to begin sorting through the anger and anxiety linked to your entitlement emotions. You owe it to yourself and those who love you to find real peace in your life.

Core Emotional Triggers of the Entitled-Spiteful Child

This is only a partial list and you may identify additional triggers. Remember, these emotions occur based on the way your Inner Child perceives a current situation. However, the kid's perception of events may be inaccurate.

I Feel Cheated	I Feel Dismissed
I Feel Overlooked	I Feel Falsely Accused
Life Is Not Fair	I am Not Respected
I Have No Voice	I Feel Threatened

Workbook

1 Do you **resonate** with the Entitled/Spiteful Child?

   Yes ☐   No ☐

2 If yes, why do you **resonate** with this child? What circumstances did you grow up with
   that left you feeling entitled or spiteful? Did this occur at home, in school, with peers,
   or with others? Write your story. Be as specific as possible.

   _____
   _____
   _____
   _____
   _____

3 What **past event(s)** in your life may have led to the development of the Entitled/Spiteful
   Child?

   _____
   _____
   _____
   _____
   _____

4 Do you think feeling entitled or spiteful is a **factor** that has driven you to engage in
   problematic addictive behaviors?

   Yes ☐   No ☐

5 If you answered yes to question 4, why do you **believe** this is a factor?

   _____
   _____
   _____
   _____
   _____

6 Which of these Core Emotional Triggers **resonates** with you?

   I feel cheated ☐   I feel dismissed ☐   Life is not fair ☐
   I feel falsely accused ☐   I am not respected ☐   I have no voice ☐
   I feel threatened ☐   I feel overlooked ☐
   Other: _____

7   Taking each trigger, **explain** why you selected it and how it **originated.** Again, write your story and be as specific as possible.

_____

_____

_____

_____

_____

8   Have you ever engaged in your addiction because you were **annoyed or angry** or felt you **deserved** to act out? If yes, explain one occasion when this happened.

_____

_____

_____

_____

_____

Learning to manage our emotions, especially our anger, is critical in this transformation journey. Anger is a primary emotion, which means it is easy to identify and engage. However, the key to controlling your anger will be determining what you are _really_ feeling. And once you identify _that_ emotion, you need to be able to express it.

Example: your wife screams at you for not going to the recycling center as promised. As she continues yelling, you get angry because she won't accept your apology. So, now you are yelling too. But instead, you should pause and consider what you are **truly** feeling. In this case, it may initially have been guilt for breaking your promise, but that guilt fades as she doesn't accept your apology.

What you are most likely experiencing at that point is frustration. So instead of a shouting match, you need to say this to her. _"I acknowledge I made a mistake, and again I am sorry. But I am frustrated that you refuse to see my remorse and accept my apology."_ There is no need for you to get angry in this situation. It will help if you learn to practice identifying what you feel when you get angry.

9 Which of these Core Emotional Triggers **resonate** with you?

I feel powerless □   I feel weak □   I have been cheated □
I have been victimised □   I am not safe □   I am helpless □
I do not measure up □   I am overwhelmed □   I feel trapped □
Other: _____

Your Inner Child needs to understand that while he/she has been emotionally trapped back in the days of past injustices, today is a "new era." And it will be you, not the child, who will run the show.

10 What can **you say** to your Inner Child to help him/her **understand** this truth?

_____
_____
_____
_____
_____

11 Well done! Now **comment** below: what two key points did you resonate with in this chapter? Be as specific as possible in your answers.

_____
_____
_____
_____
_____

Chapter 10

The Inferior-Weak Child

As clinicians, Nathan and I find it interesting the number of our clients who deal with addictions also endured severe bullying as children. Although we do not have research to confirm the correlation between bullying and the development of addictive behaviors, we certainly have observational data to raise the possibility of a connection between the two (see Figure 10.1).

Bullying has always been – and most likely always will be – a serious societal problem that leads victims to feel hopeless. Unfortunately, with technological advances, bullying is now carried out in many more fashions. Cyber forms of bullying are becoming increasingly popular among adolescents and teens. And being able to hide behind an anonymous screen makes it easier for bullies to conceal their identities. But no matter what method is used to prey upon others, bullying has a detrimental impact on its victims' physical, mental, and emotional well-being.

We have seen media coverage of children who commit suicide after being bullied. According to a study conducted by Yale University, victims of bullies are two to nine times more likely to consider suicide than non-victims. That is both a startling and frightening statistic. According to an ABC News report, nearly 30% of students are either bullies or victims of bullying, and more than 160,000 kids stay home from school every day because of fear of being bullied.

Inferior-Weak children believe they are different from other children in a "bad" way. Whether the abuse was suffered at the hands of peers, siblings, or even parents, these children find little safety in the world and struggle to trust others.

Shame is another struggle for children who have been made to feel "less-than" by others. Being labeled "weak" is stigmatising and can have negative, life-long ramifications. And while this is especially true for men, the same can be said for women who endure this type of abuse as children and teenagers. In many cases, young girls can be more abusive than their male counterparts.

"I always loved learning but hated school," said Kathleen, a 47-year-old former social worker trying to manage an on-off love affair with opiates. *"I was never attractive, and the girls at school pointed it out often. Every day from 5th to 11th grade, I cried at some point because of the cruel comments people made.*

"And it wasn't the boys," she continued. *"Some boys would try to comfort me, telling me not to let the girls bother me. But the girls were relentless. I attempted suicide on two occasions, failed, and once ended up in a psychiatric hospital for six days.*

"Today, I still have a problem being close to women," said Kathleen, who lost her license for practicing because she was under the influence of narcotics while at work. *"I would usually get high if I was going to spend time around other females. It was the only way I could relieve some of my anxiety."*

DOI: 10.4324/9781003406013-10

Figure 10.1

Feeling less-than or inadequate to your peers or siblings leaves you wanting to isolate and not take chances for fear of being called out. There is a constant worry about the unknown, fearful of where the next verbal or physical blow will come from. Many who struggle with addiction, utilise their addiction to escape experiencing emotional pain such as described here.

Kevin's Story

Kevin knows what it is like to feel weak and inferior. Raised by an abusive stepfather, this young boy had it thrown in his face every day that he did not measure up with other boys.

"My stepfather took to my older brother because they both enjoyed sports," said Kevin, 58, who came into counseling to deal with a drinking issue and porn addiction. *"But he hated me. He always referred to me as a girl because I did not like watching sports with him and my brother."*

"When I was 11, and my mom was at work, he made me put on her panties, saying a sissy should dress like a sissy," he continued as his hands started to tremble. *"He then would constantly berate me. He was a bully, and it was humiliating."*

> **"There is no need to live with the stigma of weakness that people labeled you with as a child. It only keeps you stuck in your addiction."**

But home was not the only place where Kevin faced bullies. School was also not a safe haven for him as he endured constant teasing about his small body frame. *"When I entered seventh grade, I was 90 pounds and a little over five feet tall,"* he said. *"I went to a small school, and everyone referred to me by my nickname, runt. I was shoved in lockers, beaten during gym class, and had food thrown at me during lunch. I felt worthless and inferior."*

While the bullying at school lessened when Kevin entered High School, the abuse at home was not letting up. Not only was his stepfather continuing to belittle him, but Kevin's mom and brother also joined in.

"They would say I was a pathetic excuse for a boy allowing myself to get picked on at school for so long," he said. *"I found myself isolating more and more and at 16 started drinking by stealing some of my stepfather's beer."*

After getting a part-time job in his senior year, Kevin intensified his drinking." *"I know now I was drinking to forget my life,"* he said. *"I never amounted to much of anything because I had no confidence. I have moved from one dead-end job to another all my life.*

"Every day, I had flashbacks of my stepdad belittling and mocking me or having to sit with him wearing nothing but my mother's panties," said Kevin, who, at age 58, never married. *My outlets have been drinking and porn. I have never been with a woman because I am terrified, she would think I am not manly enough for her."*

Inner Child Theory in Action

Kevin started therapy for the first time at age 58. Medical tests showed liver damage, and his doctor strongly recommended he stop drinking to prevent further erosion. Kevin started his recovery at a state-run treatment program going into the detox unit. After 45 days of in-patient treatment, Kevin was released and began his Inner Child work.

He realised that memories of his stepfather's abuse had prevented him from taking chances when it came to careers or relationships. Instead, the negative noise in his head saying he was a weak man kept Kevin stuck in his small world all his adult life.

"My stepdad was living in my head rent-free for decades," Kevin said as he recalled some key learnings from his Inner Child work. *"I allowed fear to dictate my life. And when that fear was aroused, I often turned to alcohol and porn."*

Today, after processing his abuse as a child and teen, Kevin has learned how to sit with painful emotions when his Inner Child is triggered, leading him to make healthier decisions.

"The process is so simple, but it is not easy at first," he said as he walked through the Inner Child Model steps. *"I must be mindful to recognise negative events in my life each day and determine which ones could activate my inner child. Once I have done this, I sort through the kid's negative emotions and process them. What I am doing is slowing everything down. I then take those emotions and evaluate them using rational thinking, which should lead me to make healthy decisions."*

Today Kevin is still not in a relationship but is more socially active and engaging with members of his support group. He also has been abstemious from porn and alcohol for nearly two years.

Key Characteristics of the Inferior-Weak Child

Here are some key characteristics that lead to the development of the Inferior-Weak Child.

* They are conditioned to believe they are different in a "bad" way.
* Endure bullying or being made to feel inferior by parents, siblings, or peers.
* Suffer tremendous shame.
* Struggle to trust others.
* Unwilling to take risks in fear of being ridiculed.
* No safe haven results in high levels of anxiety and depression.

Kid Talk

As you have been learning, empowerment comes when you do not act based on the raw emotions exerted by your Inner Child but instead process those painful emotions and evaluate them through rational thinking. Here are steps to deal with the Inferior-Weak Child and start empowering yourself.

* Like the other inner children we have discussed, this little one has gone through a lot of emotional and mental distress. A large part of the problem is that he/she are confused about what it takes to be accepted by others. All they know is that they feel different in a "bad" way. Therefore, part of your responsibility is to build your Inner Child's self-confidence. And this includes the fact that it's OK for a person sometimes to feel fearful and insecure.
* When your Inner Child becomes triggered, he/she needs to understand the current circumstance that is provoking the child. More importantly, the child needs to know that the situation is something you can effectively handle. The Inner Child needs to understand that the feeling of inferiority is something you can rationalise and look at from a different perspective. As you learn the child's pain points, your responsibility turns toward soothing him/her by demonstrating your ability to manage the current situation.

Core Emotional Triggers of the Inferior-Weak Child

This is only a partial list and you may identify additional triggers. Remember, these emotions occur based on the way your Inner Child perceives a current situation. However, the kid's perception of events may be inaccurate.

I am Useless	I am Weak
I am a Fraud	I am Powerless
I Don't Matter	I am a Loser
I am Insignificant	I am Fragile

Workbook

1　Do you **resonate** with the Inferior/Weak Child?

　　Yes ☐　　　　　　　　No ☐

2　If yes, why do you **resonate** with this child? What situations did you face growing up that left you feeling **inferior or weak**? Did this occur at home, in school, with peers, or with others? Write your story. Be as specific as possible.

　　_____
　　_____
　　_____
　　_____
　　_____

3　What **past event(s)** in your life may have led to the development of the Inferior/Weak Child?

　　_____
　　_____
　　_____
　　_____
　　_____

4　Do you think feeling inferior or weak are **factors** that have driven you to engage in addictive behaviors?

　　Yes ☐　　　　　　　　No ☐

5　If you answered yes to question 4, why do you **believe** these are factors?

　　_____
　　_____
　　_____
　　_____
　　_____

6　Which of these Core Emotional Triggers **resonate** with you?

I am useless ☐	I am weak ☐	I am powerless ☐
I do not matter ☐	I am insignificant ☐	I am a fraud ☐
I am shameful ☐	I am pathetic ☐	I don't matter ☐
No one cares ☐	Other: _____	

7 Taking each trigger, **explain** why you selected it and how it **originated**. Again, write your story and be as specific as possible.

_____
_____
_____
_____
_____

8 Growing up, did you feel you were **different** from other children?

Yes ☐   No ☐

9 If you answered yes to question 8, why did you **feel that way**? Be as specific as you can.

_____
_____
_____
_____
_____

10 As a child, what was your perception of what it means to be "**good**"?

_____
_____
_____
_____
_____

11 In your own words, let your Inner Child know **you have what it takes** to manage current circumstances. What would you say to the child? Be as specific as possible in your answers.

_____
_____
_____
_____
_____

12   Well done! Now **comment** below: what are two key points you learned in this chapter? Be as specific as possible in your answers.

_____

_____

_____

_____

_____

Chapter 11

The Stressed Child

Welcome to Anatomy 101. Today, we will be examining a very special hormone that serves to help us deal with stress. This hormone is cortisol. On the positive front, cortisol can increase your immunity during times of stress by limiting inflammation, which can damage healthy cells throughout the body. Cortisol also regulates metabolism by indicating how your body uses proteins, fats, and carbs and can also help regulate your sleep cycle.

When produced at healthy levels, cortisol is extremely beneficial and life-preserving. It positively impacts the nervous, immune, cardiovascular, respiratory, and musculoskeletal systems. However, on the flip side, if you deal with chronic stress or suffer from Post-Trauma Stress Disorder, your body may produce too much cortisol. When levels of this hormone are consistently elevated, it can lead to excessive inflammation, weaken your immune system, and produce a variety of health issues.

This brief anatomy lesson on cortisol is the tip of the iceberg regarding this unique and critical hormone. But the point is this – stress kills. And for stressed children, anxiety has been a mainstay in their lives starting at a very tender age (see Figure 11.1).

Melanie's Story

Presenting with an addiction to alcohol, Melanie was a 43-year-old wife and mother of two children, aged 11 and 13. One of six children herself, Melanie grew up in a chaotic household that set her up to be ruled by anxiety.

"It was mental growing up with five brothers, of which three were bullies," said Melanie, a convenience store manager who has broken off all ties with her family of origin. *"They were always fighting amongst themselves, making so much noise and wrecking the house. Dad was nowhere to be found, and mom was overwhelmed by the boys.*

"I did not have friends over because I was so embarrassed by how the house looked and how my brothers acted, she continued. *"Three of them were verbally and physically abusive to me, but I could not turn to mom for help because they treated her the same way. I always felt threatened when I was at home."*

Melanie continued to speak about the abuse she suffered at the hands of three of her brothers, including feeling sexually harassed.

"Although none of them touched me sexually, my brother Adam would stare at me, and I could feel he was undressing me with his eyes. It was so creepy, and he never stopped," she recalled, adding that she was 15 when he left home to join the army. *"And mom was always cursed at and told what to do. They treated her like a slave. We didn't tell my father because, if he was around, he was just as abusive."*

DOI: 10.4324/9781003406013-11

Figure 11.1

Melanie began drinking in her late-teenage years to escape the hell she was experiencing at home. But she found that getting high didn't permanently hide her fear.

"I got introduced to beer by some of the older boys in the neighborhood," she said. *"It was a great mental escape from the crap at home. But while my anxiety would die down when I was high, it was still there when I sobered up. So, I started to drink more often."*

"WHAT WORRIES YOU MASTERS YOU." – JOHN LOCKE

"Even after I left home, I always felt nervous, like I was waiting for the bullying to start again even though my brothers were out of my life," she continued. *"I still felt unprotected even after I got married. The only short-term escape was to drink."*

Over time, her drinking escalated, and her husband threatened to leave and take the children if she did not sober up. His threat prompted her to try quitting, but it was not easy. After a series of relapses, her husband filed for divorce. This led Melanie to take more drastic actions.

"I had been trying to quit on my own, but obviously, that was not working," she said. *"I asked my husband for one last chance, entered counseling, and joined a 12-step support group."*

After confronting past demons, including grieving her father's abandonment, her brothers' bullying, and her mother's lack of protection, Melanie experienced a decline in her anxiety.

"I haven't touched a drug in over 12 months, and I have my family back," she said as a smile appeared. *"I am no longer a prisoner in my head and know how to manage my anxiety when triggered without needing to drink."*

Through the Inner Child Model, Melanie learned how to calm her past demons and sit with the emotional pain when they were triggered. She also learned the negative narratives her Inner Child believes can be dealt with effectively without seeking to escape from them through drinking.

Stress and Addiction

In the past 40 years, much clinical research has demonstrated the apparent association between stress and addiction. In the book, *Principles of Addiction: Volume One*, Dr. Rajita Sinha of the Yale University School of Medicine describes how researchers have linked stress with addictive behaviors, including alcohol, drugs, and food.

"Many of the major theories of addiction also identify an important role of stress in addiction," Dr. Sinha writes. *"The psychological models view drug use and abuse as a coping strategy to deal with stress, reduce tension, self-medicate, and decrease withdrawal-related distress."*

He continues, *"Negative life events such as a loss of a parent, parental divorce and conflict, low parental support, physical violence and abuse, emotional abuse and neglect, isolation and deviant affiliation, and single parent family structure have all been associated with increased risk of subsequent substance abuse."*

Hidden Anxiety

Some individuals reared in abusive or neglectful environments learn at an early age how to quiet their anxiety by using three coping strategies:

* Keep a low profile.
* Do not offer to share information.
* Stay busy and be distracted.

These defense mechanisms help a child to become desensitised to their anxiety, with some reaching a point where they cannot tell it exists. However, it does. They lose awareness of stress symptoms, such as tension in the shoulder or neck area, a clenching jaw, biting fingernails, grinding teeth, pulling hair, and restlessness.

"I'd never thought of myself as the anxious type, but I do find it impossible to slow down," says Tony, a lifelong bachelor and master gardener who owns a landscaping business. He also has an expensive habit of engaging with escorts and watching porn. *"I get about four hours of sleep a night, and I go from the time I get up until I crash at night. It's just my speed – go, go, go."*

As Tony and I (Eddie) talked, I discussed the possibility of him sitting still for two to three minutes. As I suggested this simple exercise, his facial expression changed to one of shock. *"That sounds torturous,"* he said in a very monotone voice. *"I cannot do that."*

I knew then that Tony had been repressing his anxiety for decades. He was extremely stressed, but somewhere along the line, he buried his emotions and convinced himself he was unshakeable. Nothing could be further from the truth, and his go-go-go lifestyle and stress-buster outlet of escorts and porn proved the point. He cannot experience his anxiety because he is always running from it.

Buried in Busyness

Starting at a young age, Tony used busyness and sex as distractions for the anxious environment he called home. Raised by his father – Tony's mom died when he was only six – he watched his dad struggle to move on. Although there was no abuse in the home – which consisted of Tony and his father – there was little else that was positive.

Tony's dad suffered from depression and struggled to get out of bed some days. As a young boy, Tony went from having a mother who met all his needs to having no one available for him. This abandonment left the young Tony to become very self-efficient and not to impose upon his father, who had pretty much withdrawn into himself. Still, Tony worried a great deal about making innocent mistakes for fear of placing additional burdens on his dad.

"After mom died, the house died," Tony explained, who looked years older than his age of 44. *"There was no life in it. My dad and I were existing, not living. But I worried about him all the time. He was all I had left in the world. Do you know what it's like to cook your food and hope you don't start a fire or make a mess? It was not that I feared getting in trouble; I was afraid of adding additional stress to my dad's life."*

So instead, Tony took on that stress, which is a tremendous burden for a young boy. To help cope with his fearful emotions, he became active both in and outside the home. He cleaned and cooked and kept things quiet at home. He also participated in sports like baseball and basketball.

"I needed to stay busy, so I didn't think about losing my dad," he said as he continued to do excellent work in therapy, gaining the valuable insights needed to comfort his Inner Child and manage his problematic sexual behaviors. *"I learned that keeping active kept my mind off my worries and fears. It worked, and I guess it's still working today."*

But staying busy was not Tony's only way of maintaining a distracted mind. He also discovered that sex could serve as an escape to soothe his anxiety. He would spend hours looking at the lingerie ads in the Sears catalog and was introduced to pornography by friends in the neighborhood. As an adult, he escalated his behavior by engaging with prostitutes and estimates he spent over $100K on his addiction over the years.

Inner Child Theory in Action

As we continued our work, Tony came to discover that his Inner Child struggled whenever one of the following core emotional triggers arose: *"I'm uncomfortable," "I have no control," "I feel trapped," and "I am overwhelmed."* Tony also learned he never properly grieved the death of his mother because he immediately turned his focus on the fear of losing his dad.

We also discovered that Tony had repressed resentment and feelings of abandonment toward his mom, whose death had left the young Tony alone to deal with a depressed father. For Tony's Inner Child, prostitutes serve as a source of female nurturing while also providing the security of not having to get emotionally involved. He also realised he never married for the irrational fear of losing his spouse.

As he continued his recovery work, focusing on abandonment issues, Tony started to experience more anxious emotions that he had successfully hidden for years. And the more he connected with his feelings and Inner Child, the more he could sit with discomfort without resorting to escape mechanisms. Tony realised he did not have to react to the toxic emotions his Inner Child often experienced. Instead, he could slow everything down and sit with the kid's emotional pain, understanding it would not kill him. Then he could take those unresolved pain points and apply them to rational thinking (wise mind).

This therapeutic approach created a new way for Tony to manage his decision-making deficiencies. It left him making healthier choices, and over time, he slowed down his schedule and stopped frequenting escorts and viewing porn. He also started dating.

"I never realised how much stress I was dealing with and, worse yet, the negative behaviors it led to," he said toward the end of our working together. *"Now that I have faced the fear of abandonment and dealt with my inner child, I see very clearly all the defenses the kid put in place to keep me from feeling negative emotions. Looking back, it was all crazy. However, I'm glad I have come to know my inner child. He certainly is a handful."*

Kid Talk

Besides being there for your Inner Child, one of the most effective ways to assist the kid is to learn to lighten up and have fun. That's right. Enjoy yourself. Enjoy others. Enjoy life. This kid lives to escape but has spent his life doing it through addictive behaviors. Show your Inner Child there can be a healthy and fun balance in life. Show your Inner Child you are a protector.

- This is part of overall self-care critical for recovery and especially vital for the Inner Child who experienced chronic anxiety. Learn to be silly, even if you do so in private. But it would be much better to take risks and try to be humorous and adventurous with others.
- Point out to your Inner Child reasons to be grateful. No matter how complex your current circumstances are, there are still things you can point to and feel gratitude. It could be as simple as driving from point A to B and not getting into an accident. It could be that you have all four limbs or your eyesight. Appreciating the things you usually overlook or take for granted can be a game changer when reducing stress.
- Growing up in a tense environment leaves this Inner Child on the alert, so you need to help take the kid down a notch. Your Inner Child will never cease being vigilant about potential risks – many of which are invalid. It is your job to let the child know you are in control and will serve in the role of protector. You also must let the child know you will be the decision-maker when selecting the type of comfort needed to reduce stress.

You're the boss, but more importantly, you have the child's back. Stress is part of our lives. But we do ourselves a disservice when attempting to escape our emotions, especially our fears. Emotions – even negative ones – can be a source of growth.

Continuous self-reflection, obtaining valuable insights about yourself and your past, and understanding your behaviors should be a never-ending mission. Now, go forth and feel.

Core Emotional Triggers of the Stressed Child

This is only a partial list and you may identify additional triggers. Remember, these emotions occur based on the way your Inner Child perceives a current situation. However, the kid's perception of events may be inaccurate.

I Feel Overwhelmed	I Feel Out of Control
I am Going Crazy	I Feel Uncomfortable
I am a Disappointment	I Lack Confidence
I am Afraid of Failing	I am Scared

Workbook

1   Do you **resonate** with the Stressed Child?

Yes □   No □

2   If yes, why do you **resonate** with this child? What were the conditions you grew up in that left you **feeling stressed**? Did this occur at home, in school, with peers, or with others? Write your story. Be as specific as possible.

_____

_____

_____

_____

_____

3   What **past event(s)** in your life may have led to the development of the Stressed Child?

_____

_____

_____

_____

4   Do you think feeling stressed is a **factor** that has driven you to engage in addictive behaviors?

Yes □   No □

5   If you answered yes to question 4, why do you **believe** this is a factor?

_____

_____

_____

_____

_____

6   Which of these Core Emotional Triggers **resonate** with you?

I feel overwhelmed □   I feel out of control □   I am going crazy □
I feel uncomfortable □   I am a disappointment □   I lack confidence □
I feel panicked □   I feel restless □
Other: _____

7 Taking each trigger, **explain** why you selected it and how it **originated**. Again, write your story and be as specific as possible.

_____
_____
_____
_____
_____
_____

8 Do you believe you suffer from hidden anxiety after reading this chapter?

Yes ☐   No ☐

9 Growing up, what did you **worry about**? What scared you?

_____
_____
_____
_____
_____

10 Did anyone show you how to **cope with** emotional distress?

Yes ☐   No ☐

11 How did you learn to **cope** with stress?

_____
_____
_____
_____
_____

12 Do you use busyness to **mask your** anxiety?

Yes ☐   No ☐   Not sure ☐

13 What activities bring you **joy and delight**?

_____

_____

_____

_____

_____

14 Well done! Now **comment** below: what are two key points you learned in this chapter? Be as specific as possible in your answers.

_____

_____

_____

_____

_____

Chapter 12

The Early Sexually Stimulated/Abused Child

Sexual abuse is an offense that robs children of their innocence and leaves life-long scars and negative ramifications that can haunt them for a lifetime. It is a horrendous evil that can negatively shape an individual forever (see Figure 12.1).

According to the American Academy of Child and Adolescent Psychiatry, nearly 1 in 4 girls and 1 in 13 boys in the US will suffer sexual abuse at some time in their childhood. It is doubly shocking to know that a large majority of these assaults are committed by someone the child knows.

According to the Adverse Childhood Experience Study conducted by Kaiser Permanente and the Center for Disease Control, children who are sexually abused have a higher risk of developing depression, post-traumatic stress disorder, drug addiction, and suicidal behaviors later in life. They also have a higher chance of developing physical conditions such as heart disease.

Add to this, the stigma and shame that come from being sexually abused – it is enormous, especially for children who carry the awful secret in fear of sharing. Some people who have been sexually abused go to their graves without telling anyone what happened to them, while it may take others decades before sharing their torment.

Julian's Story

Julian entered counseling, presenting with numerous addictions, including cocaine, vaping, food, sex, and porn. His story is a tragic one of abuse and neglect that left him struggling to live a well-adjusted life.

Julian's parents divorced when he was nine, leaving him at home with his mother and four sisters. Following the divorce, his father ceased contact with him and his sisters.

"When dad left, mom said I had to be the man of the house and protect us," he recalled remembering the fear he felt with these new responsibilities forced upon him. *"So, I thought to myself, 'I have to grow up fast.'"*

But while Julian was trying to determine how an adolescent boy protects his family, he found himself in a situation needing protection of his own. Shortly after the divorce, Julian started being sexually abused by a teacher at elementary school.

"I had no idea what was happening, and I was informed under no circumstances can I tell anyone or I would find myself in trouble," he said. *"I left his office feeling confused and frightened, trying to push the experience aside and forget it ever happened."*

Julian watched from afar as his Dad started a new family, and he longed for the attention and love of his father, which was not to come. Instead, he often cried himself to sleep at night. Julian had to learn to deal with his emotional distress alone, as his mother was also not emotionally available. The coping mechanism he discovered was binge eating.

DOI: 10.4324/9781003406013-12

Figure 12.1

FORGETTING IS DIFFICULT. REMEMBERING IS WORSE.

"I would get home from school and immediately raid the cabinets for anything sweet or salty," he said. *"But I also had a second way to calm my anxiety – porn. I started watching it when I was 10, and it has been a source of comfort for a long time."*

Due to being overweight, Julian was bullied incessantly at school and had few friends. Early in high school, he began smoking marijuana as a new form of self-soothing.

"I developed the beliefs that 'people can't be trusted' and 'I am unworthy of love,'" he said during a later session as he uncovered the negative narratives that activate his Inner Child. To help him cope with these crippling emotions, he increased his bingeing on food and porn.

"When I was stuffing myself with sugar and watching porn, I had no worries or anxiety," he said, recalling the memories. *"With the bullying issues at school, I could not wait to get home so I could escape from the world."*

As his therapy progressed, Julian spoke of the times he reached out to connect with his father but was ignored on each occasion. *"I was desperate for a male connection – I longed for my father. But he wanted nothing to do with me. I truly thought there was something wrong with me."*

Seeking Love in the Wrong Places

When he turned 18, Julian saw an advertisement in the classifieds section of a newspaper that promoted sexual hook-ups, "mature man seeks adventurous younger gentleman."

Julian was curious and reached out to him. The man offered him $40 to perform a sexual act on him.

"I was horrified but bizarrely happy that a man had finally shown some attention," Julian rationalised his venture into gay sex. He had convinced himself that if he offered himself sexually, men would accept and desire him.

The man Julian initially hooked up with introduced him to half a dozen other older men who sexually solicited the young man. Julian, conflicted by his sexual encounters with men, used the money they gave him to hire female prostitutes and buy cocaine.

"I needed to have sex with women, just to convince myself that I wasn't gay," he said. *"But I did enjoy my encounters with those men. They made me feel cared for."*

As the years progressed, Julian got married and had a son. However, he continued pursuing the need to achieve a connection – albeit a false one – by being sexual with older men. And when he wasn't acting out with people, he was knee-deep in compulsively watching pornography in tandem with using cocaine. By the age of 30, coke and porn had become fused together, leading to devastating consequences.

"I remember I was home alone for the weekend, and I had it all planned out," he said as he remembered one of the incidents that moved him closer to hitting rock bottom. *"Copious amounts of cocaine and unlimited access to pornography. I was up for 48 hours, and my heart was beating out of my chest. My legs became so swollen that I couldn't stand up and passed out. Did I stop? No. As soon as I regained consciousness, I had another line of coke."*

Three months later, his world crashed as Julian continued to chase affirmation from men.

"I had been going to a popular gay sauna where men gave me all the attention I craved," he said. *"Until one day, my brother-in-law saw me exiting the sauna. Suffice to say, that was the end of my marriage and access to my 3-year-old son."*

As his wife filed for divorce, Julian finally elected to enter recovery.

"When you finally stop all of the insanity, you look back, and it all seems like a nightmare," he said as he celebrated his third year of being sober from coke and problematic sexual behaviors. *"I was so confused with my behavior in chasing men because I am not attracted to men. Going through the Inner Child Model, I identified my unresolved emotional pain points and processed the pain I endured as a child for the first time.*

"Now, when my father's abandonment triggers me, I reach out to members of my support team for comfort. And while I feel I need the attention of other men, what is real is I need that attention to come from healthy men."

Julian's story demonstrates how the combination of an attachment disorder (being abandoned) by his father and early stimulation to pornography (seeing what he thought was men bonding through sexual acts) can leave a young boy holding onto many confusing emotions. And this is where the Inner Child wreaks the most destruction by bringing unresolved childhood pain points into the present, increasing individuals' emotional distress levels, and driving them to escape through addictive means. The Inner Child Model helps clients identify their childhood pain points, learn to process the hurt, and how to recognise core emotional triggers when they appear. All of this helps them stay one step ahead of their Inner Child and addiction.

Sexual Abuse and Addiction

Of course, not everyone sexually abused as a child turns to addictive substances or behaviors. However, some clinical studies conducted to investigate the correlation between early sexual abuse and addiction have indicated there may be a connection.

One such study examined the relationship between physical and sexual abuse and the development of drug or alcohol abuse and found that past abuse is significantly associated with more addiction consequences. As reported in the *Journal of Substance Abuse Treatment*, the article entitled *The Relationship Between Sexual and Physical Abuse and Substance Abuse Consequences* reveals an extraordinarily high frequency of physical and sexual abuse among both women and men admitted for detoxification in urban inpatient facilities. The study also indicated that more than three-quarters of participants reported abuse in childhood.

According to the *Journal of Traumatic Stress*, 90% of women who become dependent on alcohol have suffered violent attacks by a parent or were sexually abused as a child. These findings indicate a correlation between the development of addictive behaviors and abuse – including childhood sexual abuse.

Early Exposure

We know through extensive clinical studies that consistent use of pornography can lead to devastating effects on the human brain, including addictive tendencies and sexual dysfunction. And when exposed at an early age, young minds – which are very impressionable – do not know what to make of the raw images they see. When first exposed to pornography, many children are spooked and somewhat repulsed by what they observe. But curiosity usually gets the best of them, and they return for more. And the more they watch, the more their negative feelings about porn subside. In fact, what increases for a handful of children is the desire to act out what they see.

"A significant minority of children want to emulate what they have seen in online pornography," writes researcher Elena Martellozzo in her paper entitled *A quantitative and qualitative examination of the impact of online pornography on the values, attitudes, beliefs, and behaviors of children and young people*. *"During our research, we also discovered there is a perception, particularly from boys, that what they have viewed is realistic."*

Doesn't it scare you that pornography is the predominant resource in educating our kids about sex and relationships? It certainly has us worried. Here's more on the subject.

"Studies suggest that youth who consume pornography may develop unrealistic sexual values and beliefs," writes the late Gary Wilson in his best-selling book *Your Brain on Porn*. *"Among the findings, higher levels of permissive sexual attitudes, sexual preoccupation, and earlier sexual experimentation have been correlated with more frequent consumption of pornography."*

The bottom line is that pornography teaches boys it is okay to objectify girls, and it teaches girls it is okay to be objectified. That is crazy. Worse yet, it is a recipe for creating social and interpersonal disasters for our youth.

In his book, *Treating Pornography Addiction: The Essential Tools for Recovery*, Dr. Kevin Skinner notes that boys exposed to sex at an early age may not mature emotionally as well as their peers.

"Because early sexual experiences are so profound to the child's mind, he can become fixated on sexual thoughts and feelings," Skinner writes. *"Some researchers suggest that strong negative emotional experiences stunt a person's emotional development and maturity. When emotional development slows, and the mind gets stuck on sexual feelings, a serious sexual addiction is a likely outcome."*

Skinner is dead on with his assessment. Most young boys exposed to sex at a young age struggle to become men. There are too many boys over the age of 25 running around today. So can we say the same for young girls who are introduced to porn at a young age?

The data for girls is not as robust as for boys, but the results seem to be trending in the same direction.

The bottom line is that pornography leads to a lost childhood.

Audrey's Story

Audrey was 11 years old when her stepfather started molesting her regularly. Her mother worked evenings for an import company, leaving the defenseless young girl at home with her predator. Nearly every night they were alone, her stepfather sodomised her while masturbating.

As with many children, Audrey was threatened – if she told anyone, her stepfather would kill her mother. So, Audrey went through her teen years being assaulted in silence.

"I became quite good at pretending nothing out-of-the-ordinary was going on in my world," the 44-year-old married mom of 3 said. *"I smiled, laughed, and engaged as a well-adjusted teenager. But I was always terrified. There was no peace in my life. Just endless fear."*

Audrey came to counseling after her husband discovered she had been having physical affairs throughout their 22-year marriage. Nearly all her affair partners were men much older than her. And the contact was limited to the men sodomising her while they masturbated.

Audrey was reenacting her earlier abuse, but this time she was in control by choreographing what was and was not permitted during her liaisons. Unknown to her, Audrey engaged in these behaviors to ease her chronic fears of the initial encounters. By being in control, she developed a pseudo sense of comfort in engaging in these sexual acts with men with whom she had no emotional bond.

"Most of these encounters occurred during periods of my marriage where I found myself being very fearful," she reflected. *"I could never determine what the fears were; all I wanted to do was not feel them. So, I became involved with these men to reduce my anxiety.*

"It seems so odd when I say something like that," she continued. *"You would think cheating on your husband would make you nervous, but it did just the opposite for me. My fears diminished."*

In recreating her abuse, subconsciously, Audrey was desensitising to the emotional and mental distress she experienced at the hands of her stepfather. She recalls feeling ill whenever her mother left for work as she prepared herself for another assault. It was frightening for her because she had no control over her stepfather's actions.

The sexual encounters she experienced as an adult, proved to be the exact opposite. Audrey was not afraid because she was in control of these liaisons. And if one of her partners demanded more from the relationship, Audrey would quickly end things.

"I am so disappointed in myself for the pain I caused my husband," Audrey said during a session that her husband also attended. *"I only wish I had known why I was cheating. I have always loved him and always will. He deserved none of what happened. But I understand – and I believe he does too – that I didn't do it because I didn't love him. I did it because I never faced the abuse I suffered. I let my stepfather and what he did to me seep into my marriage. And for that, I am so sorry."*

Inner Child Theory in Action – Jason's Story

Jason battled with drugs since he was 14. He came to therapy after spending ten months in a residential treatment program. When I (Nathan) started working with Jason, he conveyed the desire to understand his childhood better. He was concerned that he may have suffered sexual abuse but wasn't sure. However, he explained being troubled and confused by a specific memory where he felt naked and exposed as a child. That was the only memory he had that left him concerned that he may have been abused.

To assist Jason in gaining more clarity regarding what he had been experiencing, he was asked to draw a picture of his Inner Child using his non-dominant hand. This was done to bypass his rational, logical, and clear thoughts. The objective was to get Jason to experience and express raw emotions to understand his troubling memory better.

Jason drew a picture of a frightened young child with an expression of terror in his eyes. Next to the boy was a picture of a young girl touching the boy. After drawing the picture, we discussed it in a therapy session.

Nathan: Jason, how old is the child? What do you believe he is feeling in this picture?
Jason: He is four years old and looks terrified and frightened. He is also naked.
Nathan: Who Is with him in this picture?
Jason: That is Kayleigh. She scares him because she keeps touching him.
Nathan: How does Kayleigh touch him that makes him so scared?
Jason: She touches my anus. I feel sick. My anus feels tingly. She is hurting me.

Drawing the picture of his Inner Child assisted Jason in opening up access to memories and experiences he had long pushed aside. Drawing his Inner Child instead of a picture of himself allowed Jason to externalise the trauma and lessen the shame he had been subjected to for decades.

Now, Jason could make sense of the vague memory and recall the abuse he suffered at the hands of his teenage babysitter. By accessing the right hemisphere of his brain, where repressed memories are stored, Jason could recollect those horrific experiences. But most importantly, he could now name them and begin the healing process.

Kid Talk

If you were a victim of sexual abuse, the most helpful thing you can do for your Inner Child is to grieve as the child experiences emotional triggers that bring back traumatic memories. Remember, we are attempting to identify repressed or suppressed pain points. And that requires a great deal of courage on your part. If you find yourself struggling, I will strongly encourage you to seek the help of a professional specialising in treating childhood trauma. Talking about what you experienced brings healing.

Another way to assist your kid is to ensure the child is no longer taking the blame for what occurred. It is not uncommon for children who have been sexually abused to feel guilty and ashamed of the assault(s). Sometimes, the abuser will convince a child she was at fault for being suggestive or seductive. You must put an end to this needless and untrue emotional trauma. Use encouraging words and clearly explain to the kid that she is not at fault for what occurred – no more lies. Put the blame where it belongs – on your predator(s).

The impact of the events has made your life difficult. But real healing can be found if you are willing to apply the time and confront the ghosts of the past. You cannot continue to be a victim any longer. It is time to become a survivor. Embrace your Inner Child and let the kid know everything is ok. Let yourself know you're ok.

Core Emotional Triggers of the Early Sexually Stimulated or Sexually Abused Child

This is only a partial list and you may identify additional triggers. Remember, these emotions occur based on the way your Inner Child perceives a current situation. However, the kid's perception of events may be inaccurate.

I Feel Dirty/Unclean	I Feel Broken
I Feel Damaged	I'm Not Safe
I Feel Worthless	I Feel Unstable
I Feel Defective	I am Fearful

EXTREMELY IMPORTANT INFORMATION

One question often asked is: how likely is it that someone who was sexually abused as a child will sexually victimise others?

Unfortunately, statistics vary, but a meta-analysis of empirical studies containing a total of 1,717 subjects found 28% of sex offenders reported a history of childhood sexual abuse (Hanson & Slater, 1988). This is significantly greater than the 17% rate outlined by Dr. Mic Hunter in his book "The Sexually Abused Male."

The bottom line is that most individuals (men and women) who were sexually abused as children do not become pedophiles or sexual predators. The same can be said for those struggling with sexual addiction. Only a small segment will become sexual offenders.

That being said, the wounds of child sexual abuse should not be ignored. Please seek help if you have been victimised.

Workbook

1 Do you **resonate** with the Early Sexually Stimulated or Sexually Abused Child?

Yes ☐   No ☐

"Forgetting is difficult. Remembering is worse."

2 If yes, why do you **resonate** with this child? What were the circumstances regarding your early exposure to sex or being abused? We know this can be a very difficult topic to think about; however, it is important to face these traumas so you can break free from your addictive behaviors. Take time to write your story and be as specific as possible.

_____
_____
_____
_____
_____

3 Do you think your early exposure to sex or being sexually abused is a **factor** that has driven you to engage in addictive behaviors?

Yes ☐   No ☐

4 If you answered yes to question 3, why do you **believe** this is a factor?

_____
_____
_____
_____
_____

5 Which of these Core Emotional Triggers **resonate** with you?

I feel dirty/unclean ☐   I feel broken ☐   I feel damaged ☐
I am not safe ☐   I feel worthless ☐   I feel used ☐
I feel defective ☐
Other: _____

6 Take each trigger **and explain** why you selected it and how it **originated**. Again, write your story and be as specific as possible.

_____

_____

_____

_____

_____

7 Do you believe you have **fully grieved** after your trauma?

Yes □   No □   Not sure □

8 Have you **told anyone** about your trauma? If not, why not?

_____

_____

_____

_____

_____

9 If you endured sexual abuse, how much do you feel this abuse was **your fault**?

A It was all my fault   □
B It was mostly my fault □
C It was mostly NOT my fault   □
D It was NOT AT ALL my fault □

10 What negative messages does your Inner Child tell you about the abuse you suffered? Be as detailed as possible.

_____

_____

_____

_____

_____

11   What **encouraging messages** does your Inner Child need to hear to heal?

_____
_____
_____
_____
_____

12   List **five ways** you believe your addiction has negatively impacted your life.

1
2
3
4
5

13   Well done! Now **comment** below: what are two key points you learned in this chapter? Be as specific as possible in your answers.

_____
_____
_____
_____
_____

Chapter 13

The Spiritually Wounded Child

As you have seen throughout this book, children need safe people to talk with when they struggle with overwhelming issues. Unfortunately, many who later will deal with addiction did not have this safety valve as kids. Instead, they had to figure out on their own how to navigate difficult and sometimes frightening scenarios (see Figure 13.1).

These issues involve conflicts with siblings, bullying at school, appearance concerns, or being ignored or shamed by peers. Because they don't have many worldly experiences and are more emotionally based in their thinking, trying to manage these painful circumstances can take an enormous mental and emotional toll on children.

Having a safe outlet to share their worries and concerns is essential to lower anxiety and reduce the intensity of negative noise in a child's mind. One source children often turn to for help is spiritual leaders – pastors, priests, and rabbis – who can play a valuable role in a child's life, helping them to navigate youthful storms and challenges.

Sometimes, instead of finding comfort and wisdom in these leaders, children experience more harm at the hands of those who are supposed to care for and nurture them.

Abusing Leaders

Some spiritual leaders use their positions of authority to intimidate, condemn, manipulate, or abuse children because of their vulnerability. This can result in these children isolating themselves from the place where they should be taught that love is central to all things – the church.

The clergy and the church can have a powerful and controlling influence on families and the rules and routines adopted in the home during a child's critical developmental years. Many traditions exist in every religious denomination, including prayers, devotions, saying a blessing at meals, and celebrating religious holy days.

Throughout history, clergy and religious leaders felt called to their respective ministries and were passionate about spreading their faith and helping the needy. Their respective congregations place great trust in them, and often these leaders are given significant standing in the community and upheld as honorable and righteous.

The potential for serious issues to arise occurs when spiritual leaders are given too much power and there is too little oversight in dealing with children in their congregations. This is evidenced by the revelation of decades of sexual abuse by priests and, more recently, in some protestant churches.

Spiritual leaders are not the only ones who rain down abuse on children in the name of God. Parents and other family members also can use religious laws or Scriptures to control a child's actions. They also use guilt and shame to accomplish this.

Some parents point to biblical Scripture to persuade their children that activities such as attending a school dance or wearing jewelry are prohibited in God's eyes, seeing it as

DOI: 10.4324/9781003406013-13

Figure 13.1

lustful. *"So flee youthful passions and pursue righteousness, faith, love, and peace, along with those who call on the Lord from a pure heart,"* 2 Timothy 2:22.

Types of Spiritual Abuse

A child can endure numerous types of spiritual abuse, which lead to long-term mental and emotional ramifications. These can include the following:

- Using guilt, shame, and religious rules to control
- Manipulating by claiming to speak on behalf of God
- Holding themselves up as holier than others
- Using Scripture to justify abuse
- Non-compromising religious indoctrination
- Blaming sinful nature on a child's lack of faith
- Providing mental, emotional, and sexual abuse

Religious Trauma

The potential damage to a young child by parents or religious leaders who are overzealous in their spiritual doctrines, teachings, and rules can be devastating.

This type of trauma is so severe that it has been recognised by mental health professionals, who refer to it as Religious Trauma Syndrome (RTS). RTS occurs when individuals deal with the psychological aftershocks that come with exposure to shame-filled and guilt-producing spiritual teachings, authoritarian leaders, doctrines, and messages.

Dr. Marlene Winell is an expert in the field of RTS and the author of the book *Leaving the Fold: A Guide for Former Fundamentalists and Others Leaving Their Religion.* She defines RTS as a *"condition experienced by people struggling with leaving an authoritarian, dogmatic religion and coping with the damage of indoctrination. They may be going through the shattering of a personally meaningful faith and/or breaking away from a controlling community and lifestyle."*

Cynthia's Story

"I grew up in a home in which our parents lectured us from the Bible every day," explained Cynthia, who has been an alcoholic for 24 years, first starting at the age of 20 after she left home. *"My three siblings and I were taught the world was evil and that we should not engage with others, or they would corrupt us. We were homeschooled and prohibited from partici-pating in any social activities outside the house. We were confined to a fenced-in backyard, where we played among ourselves. There was no socializing with outsiders because that is where Satan played."*

Like Cynthia, children exposed to rigid religious environments are robbed of the opportunity to live a fulfilled life and enjoy the riches of relationships with others. And if they should ever break free to seek asylum in the outside world, they are potentially left vulnerable to abuse from those who are prepared to take advantage of their lack of social skills and, more importantly, street smarts.

"I didn't leave home at 20. I ran away," Cynthia said, looking embarrassed. *"Imagine that? A 20-year-old woman running away from home. But I did. I had only a few dollars in my pocket and didn't know where to go.*

"I was sleeping on the streets and met two women who offered me a place to stay," she continued. *"I ended up getting drunk for the first time that night. And it became a nasty habit.*

"The women also introduced me to sex, which I found incredible," Cynthia said with a faint smile. *"They set me up with a job and taught me much about life. We still live together today. But I am tired of the alcohol and need to stop."*

Cynthia described the hard-partying life she and her three roommates share. She also believed her drinking was an avenue of escape from the guilt she experienced regarding her new lifestyle.

"You see these tattoos," she said, removing her jacket to expose a sea of color covering her arms from the wrists up. *"I also have tattoos on my breast, back, and legs. I could only imagine what my parents would say if they saw me. But what they would not realise is they created me.*

"Yes, I have rebelled," Cynthia said with tears running down her cheeks. *"But they gave me no choice. I was dying in that house. And while I enjoy my life today and love my partners, I hate myself and feel enormous guilt for walking away from God. But I had to. He would never accept me as I am today."*

Cynthia left therapy prematurely, pressured by her partners, who did not want to see her experience personal growth. Just as her parents controlled every aspect of her life, her "friends" were doing the same. Unfortunately, her oppression continued.

Charlie's Story

Charlie grew up in a large Catholic family with a father who was a great provider but offered little guidance and mentorship to his son. In search of a male role model, Charlie eliminated the priests in his church who he saw as unapproachable, mean, and distanced. So, Charlie became one of the many children with nowhere to turn when circumstances become frightening. And in fourth grade, that is precisely what happened.

Charlie went to a Catholic school associated with the church he and his family attended. During that school year, an older female lay teacher fondled Charlie nearly daily. Scared, he felt he had nowhere to turn. His father was unavailable emotionally, and the priests were far too scary. They walked around in black with white collars and emoted a sense of holiness. To Charlie, the last thing they wanted to hear was a young boy claiming to be sexually molested. Besides, he reasoned to himself, they would never believe me.

The abuse left Charlie with many negative narratives, including *"I am bad"* and *"God doesn't love me."* He became an altar boy to gain some sense of affirmation and be seen as a "good kid."

Working behind the church scenes, Charlie had more exposure to the clergy, and what he saw and heard made him more confused. These men, who were held up as leaders, holy, and righteous, showed another side to Charlie, which included being verbally abusive, telling the altar boys they were sinful, and going to hell.

Feeling he did not meet God's standards because of the sexual abuse he endured and the rhetoric from the priests about his lack of salvation, Charlie battled with depression and thoughts of self-loathing. At the age of 12, he experienced pornography for the first time while babysitting at a neighbor's home. He soon viewed it multiple times a day and never thought to seek help by bringing it to his father's or the priests' attention because he had been told: *"sinners go to hell."* Charlie felt he could not tell anyone about his use of pornography.

A Life of Shame

Over the years, he entered the endless cycle of viewing porn, experiencing shame, and developing deceptive tools to keep it secret. As his use of porn continued to intensify, his self-hatred grew, and he started to cut himself as a form of punishment. He also started using tobacco and sniffing glue.

And when he married at age 24, nothing changed. Charlie continued watching porn and masturbating several times a day to distract himself from the idea that God hated him and that he was hell bound. After 14 years of marriage, Charlie's wife discovered his secret devotion to porn. It answered many questions for her, especially surrounding their lack-luster love life.

"My wife thought I was a good man," Charlie said. *"But I disappointed her just as I disappointed God and myself. She finally saw the ugliness I had been trying to hide for years. I was exposed."*

Key Characteristics of the Spiritually Wounded Child

What key characteristics explain the development of the Spiritually Wounded Child?

- Raised in a legalistic, rigid environment driven by religious rules and regulations
- Taught to have an unholy fear of God
- May have suffered abuse at the hands of church leaders
- Dealt with self-loathing and perhaps self-harm
- Disconnected from others
- May have poor critical thinking skills and difficulty making decisions

Inner Child Theory in Action

In therapy, Charlie understood his porn addiction was a coping strategy to help him quiet down the negative noise that he was a bad person. He discovered how his Inner Child is triggered by current events that remind him of his unresolved childhood pain points. Charlie was shown how to allow himself to experience the emotional discomfort he suffered in the past, including the sexual abuse. By doing so, he discovered he could handle negative distress without turning to porn.

He worked hard to identify the core emotional triggers that would activate his Inner Child and lead him to use porn and masturbation for soothing. The negative stimuli Charlie struggled with were as follows:

- I am bad when I think about sex.
- I cannot do anything right.
- I am dirty.
- I am unlovable.
- I am worthless.

During treatment, he also realised he had no idea what emotional intimacy or healthy sexuality looked like. His childhood experiences with the church, including being sexually abused, left him feeling uncomfortable and ashamed of the topic. In addition, the young Charlie also learned about sex and love by watching porn.

Charlie started to attend Emotions Anonymous to learn how to identify and express his emotions. Through bibliotherapy (therapy through reading), he discovered the keys to developing authentic sexual intimacy. We also arranged weekly meetings with a local pastor who taught Charlie the positive benefits of living a Christian life and the power of God's Grace.

Three years after starting therapy, Charlie reports he is still abstemious from porn and masturbation and feels much better about himself and his relationship with God. He also attends Emotions Anonymous and reports that his marriage is better than ever.

Kid Talk

If you resonate with this Inner Child, a high level of patience will be a critical virtue to develop. These inner children deal with significant self-doubt and guilt, which can be easily triggered if they sense someone is unhappy with them. Their ears will be ringing with the negative comments and criticism they received from those in authority growing up.

The child must also sift and understand the truths and lies regarding religion. You may need to uncover more information about God and His nature. It can help you and your child to realise God is not only all-powerful, but He is also love. He is full of Grace that He offers His children, and He accepts and loves them unconditionally. But what is so comforting is knowing you are one of His children. And you know what your Inner Child wants most – comfort. It's a win-win.

As with all children, it is vital to learn to sit with the negative emotions this child throws your way. You must slow down the child by spending time sorting out the negative emotions and processing them through the reality of your life today. Remember, your Inner Child is trapped in a time warp – your past – surrounded by negative circumstances, people, and emotions. The child intermingles hurtful events from the past with events you experience today. But in most cases, the kid gets it wrong. What happened in the past does not match the event/s happening today. And you will need to use your wise mind to clarify when the kid's barnstorm of negative emotions comes rushing toward you.

It will be helpful to point out to the Inner Child your accomplishments – no matter how small they may seem – to reassure the child that you are in control. You want your Inner Child to understand that an authority figure (you) will provide the child with a safe environment. And those decisions will no longer be made based on raw emotions but on a more stable platform of rational thinking.

Core Emotional Triggers of the Spiritually Wounded Child

This is only a partial list and you may identify additional triggers. Remember, these emotions occur based on the way your Inner Child perceives a current situation. However, the kid's perception of events may be inaccurate.

I Feel Dirty	I Feel Confused
I Feel Damaged	I Feel Unsafe
I Feel Conflicted	I Feel Manipulated
I Feel Lost	I Feel Controlled

Workbook

1 Do you **resonate** with the Spiritually Wounded Child?

Yes ☐   No ☐

2 Which of these did you **experience** most growing up?

A Manipulation ☐
B Rigid, religious family rules ☐
C Feeling unsafe ☐
D Unjustified guilt and shame ☐
E All the above ☐

3 What did that **look like**? What conditions left you feeling manipulated, bound by rules, and unsafe growing up? Did this occur at home, school, with peers, church, mosque, temple, etc.? Write your story. Be as specific as possible.

_____
_____
_____
_____
_____

4 Do you think being **spiritually wounded** is a factor that has driven you to engage in addictive behaviors?

Yes ☐   No ☐   Not sure ☐

5 If you answered yes to question 4, why do you **believe** this is a factor?

_____
_____
_____
_____
_____

6 Which of these Core Emotional Triggers **resonate** with you?

I feel dirty ☐   I feel lost ☐   I feel confused ☐
I feel damaged ☐   I feel manipulated ☐   I feel conflicted ☐
I feel controlled ☐   I feel guilty ☐
Other _____

7   Taking each trigger, **explain** why you selected it and how it **originated**. Again, write
    your story and be as specific as possible.

    _____
    _____
    _____
    _____
    _____

8   How can you healthily respond to these triggers? What **ideas** do you have for doing
    this?

    _____
    _____
    _____
    _____
    _____

9   Can you recall experiences when you were shamed as a child?

    Yes ☐   No ☐

10 If you answered yes to question 9, can you recall specific examples?

    _____
    _____
    _____
    _____
    _____

11 Well done! Now **comment** below: what two key points stood out most in this chapter?
    Be as specific as possible in your answers.

    _____
    _____
    _____
    _____
    _____

Chapter 14

The Enmeshed Child

Imagine you're driving on a six-lane highway that has no lane markings. You and hundreds of other drivers would be forced to navigate the clear, black road without guidance or direction. Where one lane starts and the other ends would be up to each driver.

You would be at the mercy of others to ensure they lined up correctly, forming makeshift lanes for the entire length of the interstate to avoid crossing into another's lane.

I am not sure about you, but that is a highway we would avoid at all costs. This word picture should give you a sense of what it is like to be raised in an enmeshed family system. No boundaries. No limitations. Much anxiety. Lots of crashes. In a few words, the environment is toxic (see Figure 14.1).

The Healthy

At the heart of any relationship is attachment. But what exactly do we mean when we say attachment? An attachment is an emotional bond shared between two or more individuals. For many people, the ability to form attachments is natural and feels rewarding. This occurs when individuals receive the necessary nurturing and guidance during the early stages of development to enable them to cultivate attachments. This critical time determines whether healthy bonding between infants and their caregivers will be established.

The critical components provided by caregivers during this early development period include the following:

- **Connection** allows individuals to accept and give physical and emotional touch and engage in meaningful relationships with others. These individuals feel comfort and reassurance.
- **Attunement** is when individuals can determine the emotional needs of others. These individuals feel confident.
- **Trust** creates confidence in an individual that she is loved, protected, and accepted by others. These individuals feel valued.
- **Autonomy** allows individuals to be independent and not intimated when making decisions. These individuals feel secure.
- **Love and Sexuality**, in which individuals understand the integration of love and sexuality, leads to the ability to develop deep, emotional connections. These individuals feel seen and known.

DOI: 10.4324/9781003406013-14

Figure 14.1

Called a secure attachment, this healthy bond makes individuals feel comfortable engaging in relationships, expressing their emotions, and being vulnerable. The positive efforts by their caregivers increase the odds of them becoming engaged in relationships that ultimately lead to the creation of healthy families.

The Unhealthy

Numerous research studies estimate that between 60% and 65% of the US population have a secure attachment. But that leaves another third of the population who do not possess the foundations required to form healthy attachment bonds. And this is certainly true of those raised in enmeshed environments.

Enmeshment occurs when there is a lack of independence between family members. Each family member melds into the next until there is no clear sense of individuality, but instead, a family unit that looks like one of Frankenstein's creations. It is ugly and dangerous.

Add inappropriate or weak boundaries into the mix, and you have a recipe that creates high tension and a suffocating environment. Children in enmeshed homes are told how they should feel or think. There is no autonomy, just the development of a groupthink mentality. The home atmosphere is rigid and driven by an overabundance of rules that must be strictly adhered to by each family member.

But the enmeshed family's most troubling feature is the loss of self. There is no encouragement for the development of individuality or distinctiveness. Instead, autonomy is eradicated, and individual growth is stifled. Children are taught to ignore their own needs to meet a parent's emotional needs. There is nothing secure about the attachment found in an enmeshed family.

Enmeshed Parent Types

In her book, *The Emotional Incest Syndrome: What to do When a Parent's Love Rules Your Life*, Dr. Patricia Love, a licensed professional counselor, highlights four parent types in the enmeshed family.

1 The Romanticising Parent
2 The Neglectful Parent
3 The Abusive and Critical Parent
4 The Sexualising Parent

The Romanticising Parent uses a child as a surrogate spouse, sharing inappropriate and intimate information that leaves the child confused and sometimes even guilty that he is betraying the other parent. This behavior is also known as emotional incest.

The Neglectful Parent forces a child to grow up and take on adult responsibilities far too early. Often referred to as childhood loss, these kids may need to care for their younger siblings or, in some cases, a parent who is ill or perhaps struggling with an addictive disorder.

The Abusive and Critical Parent is like Dr. Jekyll and Mr. Hyde. One moment the parent is being kind and sweet, and the next raging and criticising that the child is incompetent. This negative behavior may also be witnessed in the other parent, who becomes belligerent because of resentment of the child's relationship with the first parent.

The Sexualising Parent – in a large majority of cases, the child is not sexually abused by the parent; however, there is a crossing or blurring of the lines regarding inappropriate or highly suggestive sexual behavior. Again, this caregiver's behavior is another form of emotional incest.

It's a Major Issue

Each year, thousands of articles are written about enmeshed relationships and families. The topic is covered in movies, television shows, and other forms of entertainment. Why? Because watching the features of an enmeshed family unfold is like witnessing a train wreck. Although, on the one hand, it makes your skin crawl, taking your eyes off it is difficult. Over the years, there have been hundreds of books written about the subject of enmeshment, including:

- When He's Married to Mom
- What to do When a Parent's Love Rules Your Life
- Silently Seduced
- How to Break Your Addiction to a Person
- Co-dependent No More

And this is just a partial list. Hundreds of books have been written on the subject because it is a severe issue that can destroy people's lives.

Lorne's Story

Lorne was an attractive woman who, at age 28, sought help for her anorexia. When she entered treatment, this single woman, who worked as a project manager for a telecommunications company, carried less than 110 pounds on her 5′7″ frame. Starting at 16, she had been hospitalised twice for severe dehydration and once for attempting suicide. She recently moved out of her mother's home and was living independently. She had been under the care of a physician for the past 6 years, and although she reported her weight had been stable during that time, she was still far below the ideal weight for a woman her height, which should be between 120 and 158 pounds.

Lorne wanted to work on the distorted image of her body as she struggled to see herself as thin. As she progressed into her therapy, it soon became apparent that significant family issues had negatively impacted Lorne since she was a child. She was trapped in an enmeshed family.

Lorne's dad left home when she was four and her brother was two. They never saw him again. Lorne's mother did not take the loss of her husband well and dealt with bouts of depression after he left. As her therapy went deeper, Lorne described a toxic family system centered around a controlling mother who refused to allow her children to develop their own identities.

By age six, Lorne was taking care of many household chores while tending to her younger brother. She reported often feeling scared that she would make a mistake resulting in a mess or an injury to her brother.

An enmeshed relationship is not a true relationship. Instead, it's one individual standing in the way of another's personal growth.

"I think I have been on edge since my father left home," she said. *"I was being asked to do things maybe a teenager could do, but not a six-year-old. Everything centered around our mother and what she wanted. My childhood, no make that my life, was far from normal."*

What Lorne said was an understatement. Her home life was highly bizarre. Her mother did not stop breastfeeding her brother until he was eight. They slept in the same bed together since Lorne could remember and still do today, although her brother is 26.

"She always favored him, which I came to accept," she said. *"But what was hard to watch was her flirtatious behavior toward him. They would grab each other's private parts jokingly, but I think there was more to it.*

"In the meantime, my mother did the best she could to clone me," she continued. *"She dressed me in clothes she liked. She got me involved in activities that interested her. And she made it very clear that she knew what was best for me and that I would need to go with it. So I did. I would feel guilty if I tried to break her boundaries. She trained me well."*

This entwined relationship between Lorne and her mother resulted in the young girl's inability to develop her identity. She found herself entirely at the mercy of her mother and having no voice over her life. And it was this lack of control that led the therapist to conclude the actual reason behind Lorne's anorexia disorder.

As a teenager, Lorne started to manage her weight by limiting her food intake. Over time, she went from 128 pounds to as low as 100 pounds. What Lorne was subconsciously doing was exerting control in her life the only way she could – by not eating. The inability to stop her mother's micromanagement of her life was overwhelming for the young girl. Not having the power to stand up to her mother, she sought to take back one aspect of her life – her body.

"I never thought of it that way," she said after an insightful session with her counselor. *"But it certainly makes a great deal of sense. It was my coping mechanism to deal with the emotional distress of not having a life of my own. In fact, after being home-schooled, my mom selected my career as a project manager. I hate it."*

Lorne agreed with the recommendation of her counselor to start working with a dietitian to develop a treatment plan that would gradually allow her to gain weight while she continued to work on the irrational beliefs she had about her body. Over the course of 18 months, she was at 119 pounds, which amounted to a gain of more than 10 pounds. She felt comfortable with the weight gain, and her health was no longer at risk. She also returned to school to become a nurse practitioner.

"I have cut off contact with my mom and brother," she said with a trace of sadness. *"I needed to get away to start determining who I am supposed to be. I have to admit I am pretty angry at my mom. But I know I am on the right path to recovery."*

In her book, *When You and Your Mother Can't Be Friends: Resolving the Most Complicated Relationship of Your Life*, author Victoria Secunda discusses how anger emerges as children gain more insight into the abuse they endured at the hands of a self-centered parent. *"When we recognise that we are not responsible for our childhood deprivations and that we are entitled to feel anger (but not to act on it – awareness is not a license to kill), then we can let go of that anger and not be controlled by it."*

Key Characteristics of the Enmeshed Child

Let us examine some of the key characteristics that exist with Enmeshed Children and the issues they face growing up.

- You feel responsible for managing the emotions of others, especially their happiness.
- There are no emotional or physical boundaries with others.
- You care for others at the expense of your own needs and desires.
- You cannot say no to others.
- You are confused about your own identity and who you are.
- You tend to take on the emotions of others, causing severe mood swings.
- You are made to suffer tremendous guilt when you want to lean toward your own needs.
- Your parents are driven by your accomplishments.
- You have irrational feelings of guilt.
- You have no privacy.
- You struggle to make decisions.
- Your life centers around others and not yourself.
- No one encourages you to be curious and seek out your interests and desires.
- One or both parents treat you like a friend or surrogate spouse, sharing inappropriate information.
- You have a fear you will never be able to live up to your parents' expectations.

Kid Talk

If you resonate with this Inner Child, there are several major focus points involved in your recovery:

1 Find your true identity.
2 Remove the negative narratives you believe about yourself.
3 Learn to be more assertive and focus on your own needs.

Determining your true self will take time, but you start by uncovering your needs, wants, and desires. You have spent far too long focusing on what everyone demanded from you, but this is a new beginning. Your Inner Child fears disappointing people and not being proactive in recognising their needs. The child will continue to push you toward putting yourself second to everyone else. You must become highly mindful of the child's moods and begin letting the kid know that you are now in charge and can handle this new way of living. It may be difficult at first but do not let setbacks derail you. Instead, stay focused on your objective, which is loving yourself.

Getting rid of the negative voices in your head will also be a challenge as your Inner Child attempts to correct your new attitude toward yourself. Having lived through the barrage of hurtful statements and comments made when you failed to put others first, your Inner Child will struggle to believe the new positive narratives you are attempting to learn. But that is alright because, once again, you are in control of this new situation. With you leading the way in establishing the type of individual you are, the Inner Child should settle down when negative consequences do not occur. Your positive demeanor may not rub off on the kid, but it certainly will get the child to stop and notice that something is different, and with that comes a good deal of comfort.

Attempting to stand up for yourself may be challenging when you start recovery. The changes you are seeking to make will be new and unnatural for you. At times, you might find yourself slipping back and seeking to cater to the needs of others at the expense of your desires.

Building a support team you can trust and seeking assistance when recovery becomes challenging will be one of the best investments you can make. Instead of trying to determine whether your emotions are accurate or not by yourself, you can bounce them off of others who can provide you with objective and well-intended advice. You do not, nor should you, have to go down this pathway alone.

Core Emotional Triggers of the Enmeshed Child

This is only a partial list and you may identify additional triggers. Remember, these emotions occur based on the way your Inner Child perceives a current situation. However, the kid's perception of events may be inaccurate.

I Feel Confused	I Feel Lost
I Feel Unheard	I Feel Overwhelmed
I Don't Care	I'm Scared
I'm Powerless	I Feel Guilty

Workbook

1 Do you **resonate** with the Enmeshed Child?

   Yes   No

2 If yes, why do you **resonate** with this child? What conditions did you grow up in that left you feeling responsible for others and lacking physical and emotional boundaries? Did this occur at home, in school, with peers, or with others? Write your story. Be as specific as possible.

   _____

   _____

   _____

   _____

   _____

3 Do you think being **enmeshed** is a factor that has driven you to engage in addictive behaviors?

   Yes ☐   No ☐   Not sure ☐

4 If you answered yes to question 3, why do you **believe** this is a factor?

   _____

   _____

   _____

   _____

   _____

5 Which of these Core Emotional Triggers **resonate** with you?

   I feel unheard ☐   I don't care ☐   I'm scared ☐
   I feel confused ☐   I'm powerless ☐   I feel overwhelmed ☐
   I feel lost ☐   I feel guilty ☐   I feel responsible ☐
   Other _____

6 Taking each trigger **explain** why you selected it and how it originated. Again, write your story and be as specific as possible.

   _____

   _____

   _____

   _____

   _____

7   How can you healthily respond to these triggers? What **ideas** do you have for doing this?

_____
_____
_____
_____
_____

8   Can you recall specific experiences **when your parents/caregivers** overly relied on you for emotional support?

_____
_____
_____
_____
_____

9   Did you often **feel guilty** as a child? If yes, why was this?

_____
_____
_____
_____
_____

10 Well done! Now **comment** below: what two key points stood out most in this chapter? Be as specific as possible in your answers.

_____
_____
_____
_____
_____

Chapter 15

How to Effectively Manage Your Inner Child

So, what do you think so far? Have you experienced any insights on which core emotional triggers may activate your Inner Child? Have you pondered the *why* question about your addiction and its origin? Have you tried to reach out and speak with your Inner Child? Do you have more positivity for the future?

Hopefully, what you have read thus far has helped you make considerable progress. But if not, that is also ok. This is a marathon, not a sprint. As you know, it is incredibly challenging to surrender addictive behaviors.

"Addictive compulsive behaviors are attempts to feel better, so it's scary to give them up," writes Andrew Susskind, LCSW, SEP, CGP, in his book, *It's Not About the Sex*, where he provides insights on maintaining sobriety. *"It makes you vulnerable. Addictions are also used to regulate your nervous system, so it's crucial to build and strengthen new, effective ways to cope as you give up destructive behaviors."*

With that in mind, let's examine a highly effective method for engaging and soothing your Inner Child and managing your addiction. Remember, we are attempting to empower you by always keeping you one step ahead of your Inner Child and the tantrums the child may throw. Reading on, you will undoubtedly recognise some steps in the process covered earlier in this book.

The following chart outlines the six steps necessary to help you comfort your Inner Child and manage your addiction. By learning, memorising, practicing, and executing these steps, you will have the tools required to stay ahead of your addiction.

These steps are the keys to implementing the Inner Child Model. They will assist you in slowing things down, thereby reducing your risk of acting compulsively. It also will encourage mindfulness as you stay alert to negative events and the Inner Child's emotional discomfort.

The Inner Child Model is a straightforward process; however, it will be challenging to implement if you are not committed to being continuously mindful of what your thoughts, emotions, and body are telling you.

DOI: 10.4324/9781003406013-15

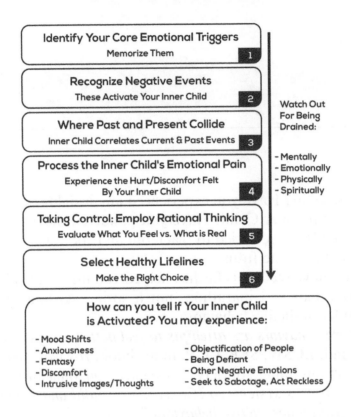

Step 1: Identifying Core Emotional Triggers

As discussed throughout this book, core emotional triggers are responsible for activating your Inner Child. This will result in your Inner Child seeking immediate comfort by having you go off and soothe yourself through your addiction.

Being unaware of your core emotional triggers makes you more at risk of engaging in compulsive behaviors. While you may not be aware of this uncomfortable state, you will experience a desire to participate in activities that distract, stimulate, or soothe.

Think about it. How many times have you reached for your phone to look at pornography or reached for another drink without giving it a second thought? Or mindlessly decided to place yet another sport's bet? These are compulsive acts we participate in without pondering potential consequences.

So what is that about?

It is about our Inner Child's struggle with the subconscious, core emotional triggers that developed in your childhood. That is why the first step in the process must be to identify and understand the triggers that activate your Inner Child.

Clients often ask, *"How do I identify core emotional triggers."* This happens when you carefully pinpoint painful and/or disappointing traumas/neglects endured in your childhood and teen years. In learning to sit with past pain – that you have long ignored – you will successfully identify the core emotional triggers that activate the kid. (It is also helpful that we listed potential core emotional triggers at the end of each chapter describing the 11 Inner Children.)

While this work is not easy, it is gratifying to trace back and correlate the events that generated the core emotional triggers which led you to seek escapes. The key is to be persistent in understanding your past and how it still negatively impacts you today. As we said earlier, understanding *why* you engage in addictive behaviors can significantly drive your successful recovery.

As you search for core emotional triggers, you must understand there could be many. Although it does happen, you will rarely have only one or two core emotional triggers. It is also important to note that you will discover that some of the core emotional triggers you identify will be similar.

For example, if "need for attention" is your primary trigger, you may find your Inner Child also activated by other emotions associated with this, such as feeling abandoned, dismissed, empty, forgotten, and inadequate, to name a few. Those emotions all have similar characteristics, but when experienced, they may *feel* vastly different.

For example, "I am unnoticed" and "I feel invisible" seem similar; however, to different people, one may be more overpowering. You will need to sort through similar triggers to determine which ones touch the most sensitive nerve. And those are the triggers you must become most aware of when they occur.

Once you have identified the core emotional triggers, you must become familiar with them. I recommend writing them on an index card or in the notes section of your phone and carrying them with you. Also, post them somewhere so you can review them every day.

Reflect on your triggers several times a day until you know them by heart. But equally important, you need to understand what each core emotional trigger feels like physically when it appears. Is there a tightening in your chest, an ache in the back of your neck, tingling in your hands and fingers, a dry mouth, etc.? Take time to determine how each core emotional trigger impacts your body. This information will provide valuable clues to alert you that your child has been activated.

Last point. The rest of the model will fail if you do not get this part of the process right. Understanding your core emotional triggers is vital to comforting the Inner Child and managing your addiction. It also begins helping you learn to be more mindful and alert. You will require new skill sets to become a transformed person of integrity.

Step 2: Recognising Negative Events

Negative events happen to us more often than we think. Most are minor, and we don't give them a second thought after a few seconds. Others, however, are more impactful and can take the bottom out of our day, causing us to crash.

Ask Yourself: Does This Negative Event...

A. Match One of My Core Emotional Triggers?

B. Does Not Match One of My Core Emotional Triggers?

This is very important: not all negative events activate our Inner Child. So how will you know the difference? Because damaging events that activate your Inner Child will involve one or more of your core emotional triggers. That is why you must be alert and evaluate all negative events against the core emotional triggers you have identified to see if there is a correlation. Following me thus far? Good.

A negative event doesn't need to be dramatic or tragic. It could be as simple as an old-time friend who cancels a lunch date at the last minute. While you may initially brush it off as no big deal, if one of your core emotional triggers is rejection, your Inner Child may correlate the canceled lunch date with a time when you were ten and you were rejected by friends. For example, you went to a friend's house and found three other friends there – but he told you he couldn't have anyone else in the house as he shut the door in your face.

The Inner Child Remembers Everything

Can you imagine the disappointment and embarrassment you may have felt at that moment? If not, rest assured your inner kid does. The child equates the canceled lunch date with being rejected by friends. Those feelings of rejection are excruciating for your child. On the other hand, you look at the cancellation with disappointment, which is a more rational way to view it.

But nothing is rational about how your Inner Child thinks and processes information. Remember, the child's thinking is emotionally based and laced with fear.

So how does your Inner Child, sensing rejection, impact you at that moment? It depends. Immediately, there will likely be a slight mood shift – and not for the better. However, as the child continues to feel more pain, you may find your anxiety level increasing. You also may start to experience emotions of defiance, sadness, or entitlement. And as your Inner Child increases your anxiety level by focusing on past pain points, you inch closer to acting out to escape the newfound discomfort you are experiencing.

Physical Ramifications

An activated Inner Child also will impact you physically. Remember, the child's core emotional triggers cause distress, so when the kid starts experiencing troubling emotions, an uncomfortable physical sensation will begin to stir within you. Being mindful of what your body is feeling can assist you in being aware that the Inner Child has become active.

"Trauma victims cannot recover until they become familiar with and befriend the sensations in their body," writes Dr. Bessel Van Der Kolk in his NY Times bestseller entitled, The Body Keeps the Score. *"Being frightened means you live in a body that is always on guard. The bodies of child abuse victims are tense and defensive until they find a way to relax and feel safe. To change, people need to become aware of their sensations and how their bodies interact with the world around them. Physical self-awareness is the first step in releasing the tyranny of the past."*

Dr. Van Der Kolk paints a clear picture of the Inner Child in his description of trauma. The kid is frightened and will remain tense until he finds a way to feel safe – by escaping into addictive activities. Your Inner Child's tension will result in your experiencing annoying and perhaps painful physical ailments. Dr. Van Der Kolk believes awareness of these troublesome symptoms is essential to overall recovery.

"Simply noticing our annoyance, nervousness, or anxiety immediately helps us shift our perspective and opens up new options other than our automatic, habitual reactions," he writes. *"When we pay focused attention to our bodily sensations, we can recognise the ebb and flow of our emotions and increase our control over them."*

"Avoid the chaos! Run away!" screams your Inner Child when beginning to experience emotional pain from unresolved childhood traumas and neglect. And that is precisely what is going on regarding your addiction. Your child's raw and troubling emotions increase your sense of discomfort while also hijacking your rational thinking skills, therefore leading you to seek comfort by indulging in your addiction.

That is why you must start with Step 1 and not only identify the core emotional triggers but imprint them in your mind. This process is about preparation. And the more you prepare for the next triggering event, the more successful you will be in conquering it.

We are not painting the kid as evil. The child is trapped in a time where he did not see rational and healthy options in times of trouble – and that mindset still is a challenge for him today. He is very fearful and needs to understand that an adult is in charge and will be his protector.

That is why it is up to us to slow everything down, assist the child in processing the emotional pain, and then take over the decision-making process by rationally thinking through the circumstances.

So, here is the big problem. How do you control an addiction when you do not know it has been activated? The answer? Learn to be mindful.

Step 3: The Past and Present Collide

At this point in the process, you can understand what triggers activate your Inner Child and lead to emotional tantrums. By reflecting on the current negative event(s) you are experiencing, you will see how the kid correlates the event(s) to painful memories of the past.

Remember the quote from Jay Stringer's book Unwanted, *"One way of thinking about unwanted sexual behavior is to see it as the convergence of two rivers: your past and the difficulties you face in the present."*

That is what Step 3 is about: understanding event(s) from the past is being muddled together with current negative events to activate your Inner Child and increase your level of discomfort.

For example, you forgot to pay the electric bill on time and incurred a late fee. This event probably is not a major negative event on a scale of 1–10, but you can not tell your Inner Child that. The child sees what has happened as incompetency on your part. *"Lazy! Lazy! Lazy! That's what we are – lazy! Lazy people make foolish mistakes!"* That is what the kid is experiencing when the late charge occurs.

Why?

Because the child remembers dad always criticising you for being lazy and constantly saying you would amount to nothing. So although you have made a good living as a police officer, internally, you feel you haven't measured up in your father's eyes. He still tells you it was a mistake not to become an attorney.

It is the heartbreak of being a disappointment to daddy that your Inner Child cannot escape. And sometimes, it only takes a minor event, such as not paying your electric bill on time, to make the kid experience that feeling of being an inadequate child.

You must embrace your Inner Child's pain even if you do not recognise the unresolved pain point the child has latched onto. All you need to understand is the kid is in pain and needs your protection.

Remember. Watch for the collision of two worlds – your past and present – because this represents an increased risk of running toward addictive behaviors.

Step 4: Processing the Inner Child's Emotional Distress

Along with identifying the kid's core emotional triggers, here is another critical component of the entire Inner Child Model process. This will be difficult because what you need to do is not natural.

Sitting in pain is like using your non-dominant hand for all tasks. It will seem frightening and make you feel clumsy and unsure of yourself. But that is ok. In time, the process will become more natural. And that is because you will find a calmness that manifests because you have a solution to the pain you are experiencing. That is the opposite of what your Inner Child experienced when he thought the pain would **never** end. That is until the kid learned to find distractive behaviors.

Your inability to sit and experience emotional pain and discomfort got you into this mess. You cannot handle the anxiety that accompanies experiencing emotional distress, and you will do **ANYTHING** to avoid it. This includes blocking out the emotions and learning not to feel. But look where that got you!

What you feel versus what is real are often two completely different things

It is ironic. As children, we mastered the art of avoiding painful feelings so that we could cope. But now, we discover that running away from emotional pain has increased the pain points experienced by us and the others we love.

If you had learned to deal with your emotional distress in healthy ways, there is a good chance you would have avoided addictive behaviors. But here you are. So, no time like the present to learn how to deal with those messy, uncomfortable emotions.

In this step, you will sit with your Inner Child and tap into the pain he/she is experiencing. Let's go back to the kid who believes he disappointed his dad.

1   First, we want to determine what emotions are being experienced. You may want to use an "emotions wheel" to help identify the potential feelings. You can access a copy by searching your internet browser. Here are some possible emotions the Inner Child feels during this adverse event: inadequate, careless, disappointed, and stupid. You will associate these emotions with the ones you experienced when you didn't pay the bill on time. Once these emotions are identified, we can move forward.
2   Now take time to reflect upon these emotions. Perhaps you will recall what it felt like when hearing your dad's harsh and hurtful words. Maybe you won't. The point is to sit with whatever emotions are present at that moment. And as you sit with the pain, embrace the hurt. It all hurts. But that is ok. Painful emotions serve a purpose.

"Vulnerability is an essential part of being human, and vulnerabilities are the doorways back into peace, joy, and love," says Mary O'Malley, author of the book *What's in the Way Is the Way: A Practical Guide for Waking Up to Life.* *"The more open your heart is, the more you have access to your natural state of peace, well-being, and ease, no matter what is happening."*

Touching the raw nerves connected to past trauma and pain is healthy, although it feels anything but pleasant when you are knee-deep in it. One of the most significant benefits of learning to feel pain is breaking free of your addiction. Think about it. You are already hurting because of the damage your addiction has caused to you and others. So, if you must suffer, why not focus on the pain that will ultimately benefit your life?

You must stand tall and face down the difficult and trying emotions that confront you at some point. If not, you will continue to succumb to your Inner Child's desire to seek comfort and escape through destructive behaviors. And when the child wins, you and your loved ones lose.

I think poet and author Kahlil Gibran said it best, *"Out of suffering have emerged the strongest souls; the most massive characters are seared with scars."*

Don't ignore your scars. Instead, use them to become the individual you always wanted to be. At the same time, you will serve as a tremendous comfort to your Inner Child.

Step 5: Taking Control: Employ Rational Thinking

So we have reached the point where we can serve to educate and soothe the kid. After sitting and understanding the depth of his pain, we will empower ourselves and ultimately control the situation.

You see, in the past, when your Inner Child had been activated, you would allow the child to dictate your actions. Then, lacking the awareness that you even had an Inner Child, never mind what motivated the kid's drive toward troubling behaviors, you gave into the compulsiveness and acted out. But now, you are empowered. You know the child exists. You have identified how the child gets activated. So, it is time for you to stop him/her from running the show. You will make that quite clear to the kid in a very gentle and caring manner.

Let us go back to the example of the disappointed dad and the core negative emotions brought on by a late fee incurred for missing a payment. In Step 4, you embraced your distraught Inner Child and all the emotions experienced with a disapproving father.

In Step 5, you take charge by letting the kid know you will no longer follow his lead and run away from this pain. Instead, you will take charge and rationally evaluate the current situation to determine if the pain felt is warranted. The conversation with the child may go like this.

"I understand this event brings back feelings where you believed dad was disappointed in us," you rationalise. *"But this negative event regarding the late fee was just a mistake. We all make mistakes, and I refuse to become disappointed in myself for doing so. Yes, it's annoying. I don't like paying the extra money, but it doesn't define who I am. So, it will be ok."*

You have taken the current negative event and put it in its proper perspective, looking at it from the point-of-view of a wise mind instead of a child-like mind. The child-like mind will always overreact to unfavorable circumstances because your Inner Child is adding past multiple traumatic events to the current negative event, making it feel more troubling than it is in reality.

By slowing everything down and reverting to your wise mind, you are communicating to your Inner Child that there is no need to be fearful. You also emphasise that you can handle these frightening situations and protect him. This will enable the child to rely on you for comfort because, as you now know, that is what the kid seeks most.

Step 6: Making Healthy Decisions

So, we come to the final step in the Inner Child Model. This is where you are positioned to make healthier choices. Remember, in the past, before you were aware of your Inner Child, the intensity of the emotional discomfort the child experienced led you to engage in unhealthy, addictive behaviors. The child's solution – I will avoid emotional distress by distracting myself – is to avoid emotional pain, which has caused havoc in your life and the lives of those you love. The mental and emotional anguish caused to prevent sitting with painful emotions is inexcusable. But it can all stop now.

You no longer need to continue to be led down the path of poor decision-making by your Inner Child. Instead, through this book, you have gained the insights and wisdom required to make healthy decisions by engaging with this process.

Returning to the disappointed dad and late fee, here is what your internal dialog may now sound like.

"Although this situation brought up memories of how disappointed dad has been with me, I am not going to do that to myself," you declare. *"Again, it was an innocent mistake. I will*

make a monthly reminder on my calendar to ensure it doesn't happen again. That will bring me some peace of mind. I handled that well. I am proud of myself, and that's all that matters."

What is the key difference between your Inner Child calling the shots and you making the right call? Empowerment. You now have confidence that you can handle situations and no longer need to escape and hide from your emotional pain. Instead, you distinguish it from past events and take control over how you will react to negative circumstances. In this case, you have elected to learn from the mistake and take steps to help you avoid making the same mistake again. When you master this step, you are entirely in charge and no longer a victim.

Please Note

Although we mentioned this before, it is important to repeat. The Inner Child Model is an extremely effective tool in aiding individuals in managing their addictions. However, you may need more assistance when it comes to dealing with all aspects of your addiction.

Perhaps you need to detox from alcohol or drugs to deal with mental, emotional, and physical withdrawal symptoms. You may need the expertise of an addiction counselor to guide you through the Inner Child Model, especially when it comes to processing past traumas and childhood wounds. And you most certainly should engage in a support group that will provide not only community support but will allow you to engage in 12-step work. Again, the Inner Child Model is just one tool that should be part of your arsenal in managing your addiction. Be sure to utilise the other resources necessary to ensure you are receiving comprehensive care.

Being Drained

There is a potential pitfall that could severely impact your ability to effectively walk through the steps we outlined with the Inner Child Model. If you feel drained in the following areas, you may struggle to stay focused and complete the Inner Child Model steps.

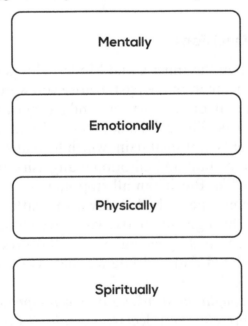

Mentally

Emotionally

Physically

Spiritually

So, what does being drained look like? It occurs whenever you become depleted mentally, emotionally, physically, or spiritually. Being drained could occur due to numerous internal and external factors you face on any given day. In fact, it is fair to say most of us walk around partially drained every day. Life comes at you hard at times, and with it comes enormous pressures. That is why you often feel extremely overwhelmed by daily circumstances. Small things you usually would not sweat over have the potential to become significant issues when you are drained.

Think about how you feel when you are tired, depressed, lonely, run-down, hopeless, anxious, or bored (to name a few). Would you say you are thinking clearly during those times? Indeed, you are not. That is because your mind and body focus on what is draining you. Therefore, you may find it more challenging to be aware of a negative event or to process a core emotional trigger that activates your Inner Child.

When you become drained, bad things happen because your brain says, *"stimulation, please."*

Because you are more likely to be reactive when drained, it is critical to be consistently aware of your mental, emotional, physical, and spiritual states. When you recognise you are becoming depleted, you will be more aware of any lurking dangers that may result in you running toward addictive behaviors.

"Be sober-minded; be watchful. Your adversary, the devil, prowls around like a roaring lion, seeking someone to devour." 1 Peter 5:8.

This is a popular Biblical verse and one that is essential for those who struggle with addiction. The lion is the temptation of addiction. However, by being alert to danger, you can take the most beneficial action to prepare – practice.

What is the game plan when temptations arise? What will you do if you feel drained? These are great questions, but you cannot wait until you are in the trenches to answer them! You need to practice what actions to take in those moments. You must determine how to stay ahead of the curve in these potentially troubling situations. If you do not, you will continue to be caught by surprise and mindlessly give in to your compulsive behaviors. **PRACTICE, PRACTICE, PRACTICE.**

For example, how do we stay alert and stay replenished? We identify potential lifelines. You can tap into these healthy resources to provide pleasant and flourishing energy boosts. Some examples are:

• Hobbies and interests
• Reading scripture and praying
• Spending time with good friends
• Working in the yard
• Taking a nap
• Listening or playing music
• Watching funny movies
• Reading uplifting books
• Cooking
• Exercising
• Calling a support partner
• Journaling
• Meditation
• Yoga
• Volunteer work

The list goes on and on. But it is essential to identify these resources and have them ready to engage when you become depleted mentally, emotionally, physically, or spiritually. If you participate in self-care regularly, you will have an extreme advantage when it comes to comforting your Inner Child and managing your addiction.

Staying Ahead of the Kid

Have you noticed a trend here? What you are doing is staying one step ahead of your Inner Child. When you engage with the Inner Child Model process, you become alert to the negative events that trigger the child. At the same time, you are involved in consistent self-reflection to determine your mental, emotional, physical, and spiritual state. Taking this proactive approach will pick up on your Inner Child's tantrums much earlier instead of mindlessly allowing them to play in the background and ultimately spin out of control. Your newfound alertness is a major key to managing your addiction.

Wrapping Up

So, we come to the final part of this recovery journey – if you elect to accept it. And that is the need to maintain self-care. This includes all the basics, such as proper nutrition, restful sleep, regular exercise, etc. But adequate self-care is absolutely everything we have discussed in this book, especially developing the practice of honest self-reflection to be sure you are truthful to yourself.

New York Times best-selling author, Bryant McGill, says, *"People who have had little self-reflection live life in a huge reality blind spot."*

You should never stop the process of self-exploration and should always maintain a hunger to learn about the complexities of your inner self and Inner Child. You also should persist with discovering all the untapped resources that can bring purpose to your life.

Because ultimately, it is through your ability to make a difference – even if it only impacts one person – that you will feel valued. We cannot begin to count the number of individuals we have worked with over the years who have gone on to work with others as counselors, coaches, mentors, and recovery group leaders after learning to manage their addiction successfully.

They have taken the pain and scars of their addiction and turned them into something that brings hope to those at the start of their battle. That is what self-reflection can accomplish. When you work to implement this process – especially when coming to understanding the complexities of your Inner Child – you not only establish freedom from your addiction but, more importantly, gain a better appreciation of life and the absolute joy it can bring.

Successfully implementing the Inner Child Model takes dedication, commitment, time, and practice. But we know you can do it. Because we did it and have worked with hundreds of individuals who have found freedom by learning to manage their Inner Child. The keys to success are in:

- An endless pursuit of personal insight and self-reflection.
- Answering the "why" questions.
- Slowing everything down.
- Understanding your child's core emotional triggers.

- Learning to sit and process emotional distress.
- Generating a game plan to replenish when you're depleted.
- Strengthening your emotional IQ.
- Engaging in overall self-care.
- Participating in community.

No matter what mistakes you have made or who you have hurt or disappointed, the final chapter of your life has not been written. This is now your opportunity to finish stronger.

Workbook

Your Core Emotional Triggers

This is where we determine the Core Emotional Triggers (CETs) that activate your Inner Child. Identifying and memorising these is one of the most critical parts of the Inner Child Model.

Step 1: Complete CET List

You will list all the CETs you identified throughout this workbook, starting with the first child you selected. Take the time to go back and see what CETs you chose for each child and list them here:

_____   _____
_____   _____
_____   _____
_____   _____
_____   _____

Step 2: Creating Buckets

You have probably noticed some of your CETs feel very similar, and that's ok. We will now separate the CETs that feel similar into individual buckets. You may end up with between two and five buckets, depending on the number of CETs you selected and how similar they are. Here is an example of how this works.

After going through the Inner Child Model, Toni came up with the following triggers:

I don't measure up	I don't belong	I feel cheated
I feel like a failure	I feel rejected	I am forgotten
I have been dismissed	I have no voice	

As you can see, some of these seem similar. So, Toni created her first bucket, and in it, she put the following CETs:

Bucket One

1 I feel rejected.
2 I have been dismissed.
3 I am forgotten.
4 I don't belong.

That left her with four CETs. After pondering, Toni decided the next bucket would contain these CETs:

Bucket Two

1 I don't measure up.
2 I feel like a failure.

Now there are two CETs remaining, and Toni decided they paired well. So, this became her third bucket:

Bucket Three

1 I feel cheated.
2 I have no voice.

The Final CET Selection

Toni's CETs are now organised, but we are not finished yet. She still has eight CETs, and we want to reduce that to a final number between four and six.

So, on to the next step: Toni will select one CET from each bucket. She will identify the CET that emotionally hurts the most when she thinks about it. If she can't decide on just one, she can select two. Here are Toni's final selections:

Bucket One: "I feel rejected" and "I don't belong."
Bucket Two: "I don't measure up."
Bucket Three: "I feel cheated."

Those are Toni's final CETs. She will memorise them and be watchful when a negative event leads her to experience one of these triggers.

Let's Give It a Try

Now that you know the six steps to comforting your Inner Child and staying one step ahead of your addiction, **let's practice**.

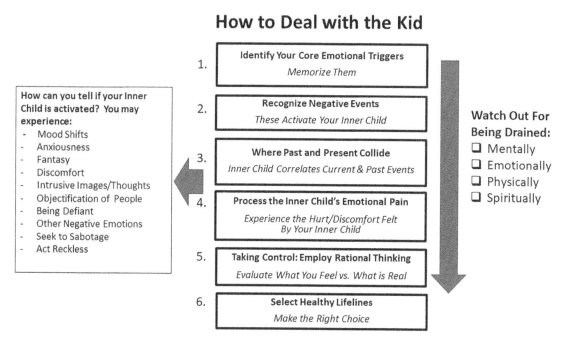

How to Deal with the Kid

1.	**Identify Your Core Emotional Triggers** *Memorize Them*
2.	**Recognize Negative Events** *These Activate Your Inner Child*
3.	**Where Past and Present Collide** *Inner Child Correlates Current & Past Events*
4.	**Process the Inner Child's Emotional Pain** *Experience the Hurt/Discomfort Felt By Your Inner Child*
5.	**Taking Control: Employ Rational Thinking** *Evaluate What You Feel vs. What is Real*
6.	**Select Healthy Lifelines** *Make the Right Choice*

How can you tell if your Inner Child is activated? You may experience:
- Mood Shifts
- Anxiousness
- Fantasy
- Discomfort
- Intrusive Images/Thoughts
- Objectification of People
- Being Defiant
- Other Negative Emotions
- Seek to Sabotage
- Act Reckless

Watch Out For Being Drained:
☐ Mentally
☐ Emotionally
☐ Physically
☐ Spiritually

Source: Going Deeper: How the Inner Child Impacts Your Sexual Addiction.
Inner Child Model –Abundant Life Counseling, NC

Step 1: Identifying CETs

Select one CET you identified that stands out to you as especially powerful.
   Example: *"I am a disappointment."*

Step 2A: Recognising Negative Events

Identify a possible negative event that could lead to this trigger activating your Inner Child.
   Example: *"I forgot to pay the phone bill."*

Step 2B: Being Mindful of Your Body

While not listed as a step in the chart, this is critical to staying one step ahead of your addictive behaviors. Be still and try to notice any uncomfortable physical sensations, thoughts, or mood shifts that could be produced by the negative event you identified.
   Example: *"My gut hurts; I feel scared; I am sweating."*

Step 3: The Past and Present Collide

Explore the reasons why this negative event might be activating your Inner Child. Can you think of a time when you felt disappointed as a child?
   Example: *"My father constantly told me I could do nothing right."*

Step 4: Processing the Child's Emotional Pain

Don't ignore your scars. Allow yourself to be present with your Inner Child and feel the pain – in this case, disappointment for the bill not being paid. The Inner Child also recalls dad's sharp words of discouragement.

This is the step that, until now, would lead you to run away and escape by using addictive behaviors. The key is to sit with your emotional discomfort and feel the hurt of dad's words. This step can last a few minutes to hours, depending upon the extent of the unresolved childhood pain point. The key is not to run away but to stay present with the pain.

   Example: *"My heart breaks for my Inner Child as I think of what we experienced by father being so harsh. He should have understood us more and helped us learn instead of being critical."*

Step 5: Taking Control: Employ Rational Thinking

In this step, we will move away from our emotional thinking, which is driven by the Inner Child and leads us to act out. Instead, we shift gears to become more rational in our thought processes. You will educate and soothe your Inner Child, taking control to help him/her understand that you do not have to run away from the distress you are experiencing. Instead, you will manage the Inner Child by rationally evaluating the situation as an adult.

   Example: *"Yes, I feel bad that I did not pay the bill on time and got hit with the late fee, but it was just a mistake. I am usually very responsible when it comes to paying the bills. I have no reason to beat myself up. Instead, I know in the future, I just need to be more aware of due dates."*

Step 6: Making Healthy Decisions

In this final step, you will take action to handle the situation wisely, making you feel proud of yourself.

Example: *"Moving forward, I will put a reminder on my calendar listing due dates for all my bills. I am not going to feel shamed by this mistake."*

Well done! You just successfully implemented the Inner Child Model.

Memorising the Steps

Now the aim is to memorise these steps, and you can do this by using just two words for each step. There is no need to memorise Step 1: Identifying CETs, as you have already done this. So, here are the two words to help you recall each of the remaining steps:

Step 2: Negative Event
Step 3: Worlds Collide
Step 4: Emotional Discomfort
Step 5: Rational Thinking
Step 6: Healthy Choice

If you prefer, come up with your memorisation technique. The critical point is to learn these steps inside out so you don't get blindsided when a negative event occurs.

The Being Drained Trap

As discussed in this chapter, a potential pitfall that could severely impact your ability to walk through the steps effectively is becoming drained. So, what does becoming drained look like for us? In a nutshell, it is whenever you get depleted:

• Mentally
• Emotionally
• Physically
• Spiritually

Becoming drained could occur due to a multitude of internal and external factors we face on any given day. In fact, it is fair to say most people walk around partially drained daily. Life comes at us hard at times, and sometimes with enormous pressures. That is why we often feel overwhelmed by the circumstances we face daily.

Think about how you feel when you are tired, depressed, lonely, run-down, anxious, hopeless, or bored (to name a few). Would you say you are thinking clearly during those times? Indeed, you are not. That is because your mind and body focus on what is draining you. As a result, you may find it more difficult to notice a negative event or process the CET activating your Inner Child.

When we become drained, bad things happen because our brains scream, *"Stimulation, please!"*

Since we are more likely to be reactive when drained, we need to be aware of our mental, emotional, physical, and spiritual states. When we know that we are getting depleted, we can also become more alert to lurking dangers.

What is your game plan when temptations arise? What will you do if you feel drained? These are great questions, but you can't afford to wait until the circumstances arise to answer them. You must practice your actions and work out how to stay ahead of the curve in these potentially troubling situations. If you don't plan for it, you will continue to be caught by surprise and mindlessly give in to your compulsive behaviors. **PRACTICE, PRACTICE, PRACTICE**.

You practice by taking time each day to walk through the Inner Child Process and what actions you should take when temptation occurs. You also should take two to three minutes several times a day to determine how you are doing mentally, emotionally, physically, and spiritually. You cannot wait until you are in the trenches to plan your response to the problematic circumstances that await you. You must have an action plan that is ready to launch.

And if you find yourself drained, you need to get replenished. We do this by identifying potential **Lifelines**. You can tap into these healthy resources to provide pleasant and flourishing energy boosts. Refer to question 2 below for a list of examples.

1 **What drains you?** What are the main reasons you feel mentally, emotionally, physically, or spiritually drained?

_____

_____

_____

_____

_____

2 Which of the following **healthy Lifelines** can replenish you when you are drained?

☐ A. Hobbies
☐ B. Reading
☐ C. Spending time with friends
☐ D. Listening to or playing music
☐ E. Watching funny movies
☐ F. Reading uplifting books
☐ G. Exercising
☐ H. Journaling
☐ I. Cooking
☐ J. Yoga
☐ K. Meditation
☐ L. Volunteer work
☐ M. Other: _____

Appendix
Inner Child Exercises

How to Connect with Your Inner Kid

During therapy, we utilise many exercises with our clients to assist them in accessing and managing their Inner Child. While we strongly recommend these exercises should be completed with a therapist, they can be used alone by an individual. Pick and choose the exercises you feel most comfortable attempting.

Exercise 1: A Letter from Your Inner Child

The letter is an open invitation to your vulnerable Inner Child to emerge and communicate with you. When doing this exercise, you should use your **non-dominant hand**. This will allow you to access emotions beyond your logical and inner thoughts, permitting your Inner Child to talk to you directly.

Here is an example of a letter written by Paul's Inner Child:

Dear Big Paul, please, please help me. I am scared and all alone. You no longer provide me comfort by using alcohol to escape, and I don't know what to do with this pain I feel. I need you! Little Paul.

This is a brief example of how a letter may start. As you focus on the emotional pain points from your childhood, you will learn more about your Inner Child. This practical exercise begins a dialog with the Inner Child, which is critical for healing.

Exercise 2: Letters to the Cast of Characters

With brutal honesty, this exercise allows you to convey the thoughts and feelings of your childhood to all the individuals who played a role in your story. This could be a mom, dad, sibling, aunt, bully, or an authority figure – any person who harmed your development in childhood and adolescence.

Here is an example of a letter Michelle wrote to her mother.

Dear Mom,

Over the years that I've been alive, you have never shown me unconditional love. You have always been very cold and distant and always wanted me to do the things "you" thought were best for me – which I never enjoyed. You chose alcohol over me and left me to bring up my brother – when I was still only a child. You told me I was 'useless, pathetic, inferior, and would never amount to anything.' I took these beliefs into my adulthood, and they've significantly impacted my inability to find happiness. I believed 'I wasn't good enough,' which has held me back from pursuing my hopes and dreams.

I know you had a horrible childhood, and I can understand why you behaved the way you did. You were never equipped to be a mother. I don't hate you, I just want you to know the damage you inflicted on me during childhood.

I do want to take a moment to thank you. Thank you for teaching me to be strong and showing me how not to raise children. I will give my kids the childhood I wish you had given me.

Today, you no longer live in my head rent-free. I am making a stand – I will be me.

The purpose of this exercise is not about making peace with your cast of characters – it's about creating harmony within yourself. This is an intense and powerful exercise, and the catharsis that transpires will start you on the long journey to healing from your emotional pain points and past trauma.

Michelle was relatively tame in communicating with her mother and offered some praise. Your letters do not need to take that same approach. You can share raw and unfiltered emotions. Again, these letters are designed to allow you to release your frustration, sadness, and anger in a positive manner.

Exercise 3: Nurturing Your Inner Child

This exercise is focused on helping you to demonstrate empathy and compassion towards the Inner Child. First, gather old photographs from your childhood and scatter them around you. As you review the photos, take notice of yourself as a child. What do you see beneath any smiles you may have had in the photos? Are you smiling? Are others in the images smiling?

Attempt to recall some of the issues you may have been facing at that time. What emotions were you dealing with at that age? Is it possible to imagine that the child in the photo is your frightened Inner Child?

Today as an adult, standing next to that child, what words and actions would you use to soothe and comfort them? Start talking to the wounded Inner Child and explain how things were back then at home, using details from your childhood.

For example, you may say:

"I know dad was never around. You (your Inner Child) thought dad must not like you because he never wanted to spend time with you. But that wasn't your fault. Dad was an alcoholic and struggling with his addiction, there is nothing you could have done. It wasn't your fault, and it's important to know nothing is wrong with you. I am here for you now."

By nurturing your Inner Child, you can validate the child's needs, learn to express emotions healthily, increase your self-compassion, and develop self-love. All of these are essential for healing from past trauma. But remember, the kid is not going away. Although you may settle him down today, he can pop back again tomorrow, throwing another trauma.

Exercise 4: Uncovering Your Inner Child's Fears

Your Inner Child grew up with no control over the circumstances she faced as a kid. It's essential to understand what fears your Inner Child faces and how you can offer protection from them.

Part one of this exercise asks your Inner Child what fears the child endures. Again, it is critical to use your **non-dominant hand** to record the kid's answers. Do not rush this part of the exercise. Take your time, and if needed, complete the exercise over the course of several days.

After evaluating your Inner Child's responses, you are ready for part two of the exercise. Based on the child's answers, what you will do is write a letter to the kid letting her know how you will work to protect her from her fears. Again, take your time, and be convincing. Remember, the Inner Child has difficulty trusting people, so you must make your promises strong and credible.

Moving forward, you will review your promises and commitments on a regular basis so that you can keep them at the top of your mind. Your Inner Child wants comfort, which can be achieved by knowing that you are in charge and have everything under control.

Exercise 5: Rescue Scene

This exercise is used to help individuals who have suffered physical, emotional, psychological, and sexual abuse. Firstly, draw a picture of the traumatic event. Then, draw a picture of the 'adult you' saving your inner child from the abuse. The purpose of this exercise is not to diminish the abuse you suffered, but alter the memory, as each time the traumatic event is recalled in the future, it will be remembered with the rescue scene. This will stop you retraumatizing yourself time and time again. This has proven hugely effective with our clients and an essential exercise to promote the healing process.

Exercise 6: Loving on Your Child

You will need a poster board for this exercise, where the objective is to reap praise on your Inner Child. You can use photos from magazines, inspiring quotes, poetry, musical lyrics, etc., to create the board. Highlight some of the child's talents and positive attributes. If you struggle to identify any, that demonstrates how harsh and unforgiving you are on yourself.

Everyone has positive qualities and talents. If you have not recognised yours, sit with a trusted friend or family member to get their input and insights. You may also want to think about yourself as a young child. What were some of the activities you enjoyed the most? Did you have dreams of what your life would be like? What would bring a smile to your face?

Once you gather this information, return to creating the praise board. When you are finished, put the board in a place where you can see it regularly. Several days a week, reflect on the board and repeat words of praise to your Inner Child.

References

Armstrong, Eric. *The Nature of Sexual Addiction*. www.TreeLight.com. 2004.

Bader, Michael J. *Arousal: The Secret Logic of Sexual Fantasies*. St. Martin Press. 2002.

Bauman, Andrew J. *The Psychology of Porn*. Independently published. 2018.

Bradshaw, John. *Homecoming: Reclaiming and Healing Your Inner Child*. Bantam Books. 1990.

Carvalho, Esly R. *Healing the Folks Who Live Inside*. EMDR Treinamento e Consultoria Ltda. 2013.

Colbert, Ty. *Broken Brains or Wounded Hearts*. Kevco Pub. 1996.

Diamond, Stephen A., Ph.D., Psychology Today (Online Version). *Essential Secrets of Psychotherapy: The Inner Child*. June 7, 2008.

Franklin, DeVon. *The Truth about Men*. Howard Books, New York. 2018.

Hunter, Mic. *The Sexually Abused Man*. Vol. 1. Jossey-Bass Pub. 1990.

Love, Patricia. *The Emotional Incest Syndrome: What to do When a Parent's Love Rules Your Life*. Bantam Press, London. 1991.

Martino, Anthony. *The Inconsequential Child: Overcoming Emotional Neglect*. Vangelo Media. 2015.

O'Malley, Mary. *What's in the Way Is the Way: A Practical Guide for Waking Up to Life*. True Sounds, Boulder, CO. 2016.

Price, Donald, Ph.D. *Inner Child Work: What Is Really Happening. Dissociation*. Vol. IX, No. 1, March 1996.

Price, Matt. *Inner Child: Find Your True Self, Discover Your Inner Child and Embrace the Fun in Life*. Self-published. 2014.

Solomon, Stacey M. *Childhood Loneliness: Implications and Intervention Considerations for Family Therapists*. The Family Journal: Counseling and Therapy for Couples and Families. April 2000.

Skinner, Kevin B. Ph.D. *Treating Pornography Addiction: The Essential Tools for Recovery*. Growth Climate Inc., Provo, Utah. 2005.

Stringer, Jay. *Unwanted. How Sexual Brokenness Reveals Our Way to Healing*. NavPress. 2018.

Susskind, Andrew. *It's Not about the Sex*. Central Recovery Press. 2019.

Van Der Kolk, Bessel, M.D. *The Body Keeps the Score: Brain, Mind, and Body in the Healing of Trauma*. Penguin Books. 2015.

Webb, Jonice. *Running on Empty*. Morgan James Publishing. 2016.

Winell, Marlene. *Leaving the Fold: A Guide for Former Fundamentalists and Others Leaving Their Religion*. New Harbinger Publications. 1994.

Yerkovich, Milan, Yerkovich, Kay. *How We Love: Expanded Edition*. WaterBrook Publishing. 2017.

Index

Note: Page numbers in *italics* refer to figures.

For Product Safety Concerns and Information please contact our EU
representative GPSR@taylorandfrancis.com Taylor & Francis Verlag GmbH,
Kaufingerstraße 24, 80331 München, Germany

Printed and bound by CPI Group (UK) Ltd, Croydon, CR0 4YY
08/06/2025
01897013-0003